The Tokyo Round of Multilateral Trade Negotiations

A Case Study in Building Domestic Support for Diplomacy

The
Tokyo Round
of
Multilateral
Trade Negotiations

A Case Study in Building Domestic Support for Diplomacy

Joan E. Twiggs

Foreword by Robert S. Strauss

UNIVERSITY
PRESS OF
AMERICA

LANHAM • NEW YORK • LONDON

INSTITUTE FOR THE
STUDY OF DIPLOMACY

GEORGETOWN UNIVERSITY

University Press of America,® Inc.

4720 Boston Way
Lanham, MD 20706

3 Henrietta Street
London WC2E 8LU England

British Cataloging in Publication Information Available

Printed in the United States of America

Co-published by arrangement with
the Institute for the Study of Diplomacy,
Georgetown University

Library of Congress Cataloging in Publication Data

Twiggs, Joan E.
    The Tokyo round of multilateral trade negotiations.

    Bibliography: p.
    1. Tokyo Round (1973-1979)   2. Foreign trade
regulation.   3. Tariff—Law and legislation.   4. United
States—Foreign relations—1945-   .   I. Title.
K4603 1973.T95   1987   382.9'1   86-24738
ISBN 0-8191-5776-7 (alk. paper)
ISBN 0-8191-5777-5 (pbk. : alk. paper)

All University Press of America books are produced on acid-free
paper which exceeds the minimum standards set by the National
Historical Publications and Records Commission.

Contents

Foreword

Robert S. Strauss

THE TOKYO ROUND of Multilateral Trade Negotiations (MTN) that meant so much to the preservation and advancement of the international trading system was, among other things, an exercise in domestic American politics at its best. In fact, during my tenure as Special Trade Representative (STR), I spent as much time negotiating with domestic constituents (both industry and labor) and members of the U.S. Congress as I did negotiating with our foreign trading partners. This experience taught me that trade policy, while certainly requiring full participation and leadership by trade policy specialists and theorists, cannot be made by them alone. It requires a healthy dose of political realism. In fact, I think that this is also true for any other area of international diplomacy. The excellent monograph by Joan Twiggs which follows is an important contribution to the literature analyzing the MTN because it places this process in its proper context.

Our experience with the MTN holds important lessons for American foreign policy officials. Too often, the role of Congress and the public in formulating foreign policy has been disparaged. There is a view among many that foreign policy (including trade policy) should be made by professional diplomats and foreign policy (or trade policy) experts, removed from the political process. It is an attitude that foreign policy should not be tainted by the "special interests" of the American public and the "politics" of the U.S. Congress. Such thinking has contributed on more than one occasion to negative results when positive achievements seemed within reach. Time and again, our diplomats have achieved substantial accomplishments at the negotiating table only to have their final product rejected by the Congress and the American people. A political constituency must always be developed to support negotiating progress.

During the Tokyo Round negotiations, my colleagues and I undertook an extensive program to inform various constituent groups around the country as to the significance and benefits of the negotiations. Ambassadors Alan Wolff and Alonzo McDonald were splendid partners. There were hundreds of speaking engagements around the country. We spoke in Illinois and South Dakota, as well as California and New York. We, and others of the staff, covered the country from the Southeast to the West Coast, and from New England to Texas. In this way we were able to greatly increase the level of awareness around the country regarding the negotiations. Of course, our objective was not simply to create a better educated public; we set out to develop broad support for the end product. We pointed out the broad array of important national economic interests involved. It was essential to convince people throughout the country that the Tokyo Round involved them and was in their best interests if it was to have a chance to be approved by the Congress in a protectionist climate.

In any negotiating process you can't make progress without being willing to give something up, and this adds to the political problem. There must be economic losers, as well as winners, in any trade negotiations. Ultimate success must be measured, when it's all added up, by whether or not there are net economic benefits from the final agreement. For instance, during the MTN it was necessary to make concessions that would affect the domestic alcohol industry (i.e., wine gallon/proof gallon). It was necessary to reduce the level of protection for the alcohol industry in order to gain certain concessions from our trading partners in other sectors. This could have become a most bitter issue. It was, quite understandably, objected to by segments of our liquor industry. However, this example illustrates the way in which we managed to strike a political balance in the course of the negotiations. In spite of our concessions on alcohol, Kentucky's congressional delegation eventually supported the MTN and the implementing legislation because we were able to gain concessions of substantial value to Kentucky's economy in other areas. We made a point of negotiating vigorously for concessions on trade in tobacco and on other items. As a result, the Kentucky delegation came to realize that the state would benefit, on balance, from the MTN agreements. The Kentucky congressional group was a strong and able delegation, keenly concerned about the national interest, but they also had to protect the interests of their state.

With respect to private industry, we employed the formal consultative process involving regular meetings with the Industry Sectoral Advisory Committees, as well as numerous informal meetings with various business and labor leaders and trade association representatives. This process was important not only in developing support for the negotiations, but also in helping us to better understand America's economic needs and interests in the many trade issues under consideration. They, of course, understood their own sectors better than we. We could not have adequately defined our own negotiating objectives without these frequent consultations. It was a mutually beneficial process.

Our congressional strategy encompassed leaders in both the House and Senate, and was directed at both political parties. Senator Russell Long (then chairman of the Senate Finance Committee) and Senator Abraham Ribicoff (then chairman of the Finance Committee's Trade Subcommittee) were two of the key players whose support was essential to success. After we had made substantial progress, we were able to convince them to go to Geneva, where the negotiations were being held. They spent two days there, and the STR staff there devoted considerable time and energy to a series of comprehensive briefings. In this way they came to understand that the negotiations were proceeding smoothly, and that the MTN would be extremely beneficial to the United States if it could be successfully concluded. As a result, Senators Long and Ribicoff became perhaps our most significant supporters in the United States Congress. They stuck with the process from beginning to end, until the implementing legislation was passed.

At the same time, we were able to cultivate significant support on the Republican side of the aisle. Bipartisan support is an essential component in all areas of U.S. foreign policy. While not always possible, policymakers should at least exhaust every avenue to attempt to forge a bipartisan consensus. For instance, Senator William Roth, a Republican with a long-standing involvement in trade issues, became extremely committed and was a great asset, and he spent a great deal of time following the negotiations.

In the House, we employed an equally broad-based strategy. Perhaps the central supporter of the Tokyo Round in the House was Representative Charles Vanik of Ohio (then chairman of the Trade Subcommittee of House Ways and Means). Congressman Vanik had become a central player in the House on issues of trade policy, and he was involved in most significant trade issues even beyond the Tokyo Round negotiations. His support of the Tokyo Round became the linchpin for our efforts to maintain support in the House. However, as in the Senate, we did not neglect the Republican minority. Both Representatives Barber Conable and William Frenzel were informed and politically effective vital supporters.

Of course, it was necessary not only to obtain support of key committee chairmen, but also to involve the Democratic and Republican leadership of both houses. Again, we were able to gain support by illustrating the American interests at stake in these negotiations. After one briefing, Republican Congressman John Rhodes stood up and said, "Well, Bob, go back and worry about your Democrats, we'll deliver a higher percentage of votes than the Democrats do." The MTN became a matter on which members of Congress, having been properly briefed, exhibited considerable statesmanship and leadership.

Of course, congressmen cannot always be convinced by a demonstration of the broader national interests involved in a given matter. Time and time again, we had to show the delegations of various states how their constituents would benefit by the successful conclusion of the Tokyo Round. This required extensive homework, a lot of patience and numerous meetings. Fortunately, these efforts, which paralleled our negotiations, paid off.

Labor played a constructive role because certain key union presidents were kept deeply involved; and, after we got them involved, they realized they had a big a stake in the negotiations. We briefed them regularly, and they saw that the national interests, as well as their own interests, were being served.

The MTN process was an almost classic example of demonstrating the legitimate and vital role to be played by Congress and the public in international negotiations. As it turns out, making members of Congress and private citizens active partners in the process did not taint the negotiations. Rather, this partnership enabled us to define American negotiating objectives more clearly. Of course, we could not give everyone what they wanted, and we often had to be the arbiters of competing domestic interests. In addition, we were sometimes unsuccessful in achieving our negotiating objectives.

In the end, we found that our efforts to build a political constituency at home and our efforts to negotiate with our trading partners merged into a single two-way process which overcame the natural hesitancy of many domestic groups to endorse international trade negotiations, particularly where they involved wide-ranging concessions by the United States and occurred during a time of rampant protectionism. Obviously, it would have all been for naught if the implementing legislation had not been passed. It was equally significant that the consultative process made the negotiations more open and, in a sense, more democratic. We, as trade negotiators for the United States, really had to sit and listen to many points of view, reflecting the views of industry and labor, of all political persuasions and all regions of the country. As a result, at the final stage the implementing legislation for the Tokyo Round trade agreements was passed overwhelmingly by both the House and the Senate. The study by Joan Twiggs is a first-rate presentation of this American project. It is particularly timely today.

Preface

ETWEEN 1965 AND 1981, the United States was involved in
the negotiation of four major international agreements.
Each one, upon completion, required the approval of the
Congress.

One, the SALT II Treaty, was never brought to a vote. A
second, the Law of the Sea Treaty, was repudiated by the Reagan
administration before it was ever submitted to the Congress. A
third, consisting of the Panama Canal Treaties, was ultimately
ratified, but only after a bitter congressional struggle and further
negotiations with Panama.

Only one set, the agreements that followed the Tokyo Round of
multilateral trade negotiations, sailed through Congress with a
minimum of opposition.

While the repudiation of agreements and treaties by the
Congress is not new, it has happened with greater frequency in
recent years. The experience casts serious doubt on our capacity
as a nation to conclude and accept significant agreements with
other nations.

The Tokyo Round agreements appear to be an exception. This
study seeks to understand why. It seeks to answer the question
whether there are lessons from the experience of these agreements that can be applied to other types of diplomatic negotiation.

The Institute for the Study of Diplomacy acknowledges with appreciation the support of this study by the Exxon Education Foundation.

* * * * *

The following individuals were consulted in the course of preparing this manuscript. They were enormously helpful in providing information and viewpoints, suggesting others to contact, and reviewing drafts of manuscripts.

Ambassador Robert S. Strauss, U.S. Special Trade Representative, 1977–79

Ambassador Alonzo L. McDonald, Deputy U.S. Special Trade Representative and head of delegation in Geneva for the Tokyo Round

Ambassador Alan William Wolff, Deputy U.S. Special Trade Representative in Washington during the Tokyo Round and acting head of delegation in Geneva in 1975

I.M. Destler, Institute for International Economics

Richard Rivers, Akin, Gump, Strauss, Hauer and Feld; general counsel, Office of the Special Trade Representative, during the Tokyo Round

Robert C. Cassidy, Jr., Wilmer, Cutler and Pickering; formerly senior staff person, Senate Finance Subcommittee on International Trade

Senator Abraham Ribicoff, former chairman, Subcommittee on International Trade, Senate Finance Committee

Harry T. Lamar, consultant; formerly House Ways and Means Trade Subcommittee Staff

David B. Rohr, Commissioner, International Trade Commission; formerly Ways and Means Trade Subcommittee staff and Commerce Department

Phyllis Bonanno, Office of the United States Trade Representative

Dr. Irene Meister, American Paper Institute

Bernard Falk, National Electrical Manufacturers

John Hudson, United States Department of Agriculture

Robert Harper, United States Department of Agriculture

Carolyn Entwhistle, United States Department of Agriculture

Glen D. Hofer, National Council of Farmer Cooperatives

Leonard Lobred, National Food Processors Association

Frederick L. Montgomery, Office of the United States Trade Representative, formerly of the Commerce Department

William K. Krist, Office of the United States Trade Representative, formerly of the Commerce Department

Louis J. Murphy, United States Department of Commerce

Betsy White, United States Department of Labor

Ann Ryder, United States Department of Commerce

Douglas Newkirk, Office of the United States Trade Representative

William E. Barreda, United States Department of the Treasury

Lloyd Hackler, National Retailers Association

Stanley J. Heginbotham, Congressional Research Service, Library of Congress

Raymond Ahearn, Congressional Research Service, Library of Congress

The Tokyo Round of Multilateral Trade Negotiations

A Case Study in Building Domestic Support for Diplomacy

1

Regulating Trade in the Postwar Era

O N JULY 26, 1979, PRESIDENT JIMMY CARTER signed into law the Trade Agreements Act of 1979, implementing the results of the Tokyo Round of trade negotiations held in Geneva between 1973 and 1979. The Tokyo Round was the seventh in a series of trade negotiations since the multilateral system was established in 1947. More than one hundred countries participated. Issues under discussion involved tariff and nontariff barriers to trade in industry and agriculture.

These are bread-and-butter issues for the average American. They involve jobs and prices and freedom of the marketplace, and would seem as close to citizens as issues involved in political negotiations. It would seem to follow that the results of a trade negotiation would face as uncertain a political process as do agreements on arms control, the Panama Canal or other political matters.

At the time the Tokyo Round began, moreover, the country was facing the pressures of protectionism because of a declining competitive position; the world economy had been rocked by the oil shock of 1973; and the international trade picture was complicated by the growing strength of the European Community and Japan. The international consensus that had been developed to launch the round threatened to unravel on a number of occasions, and negotiators spoke of taking a "mini-harvest" of very modest tariff reductions and concluding.

Controversy in trade policymaking is expected. Decisions involve a reconciliation of domestic economic interests with international economic and foreign policy concerns. The United States must make concessions as well as request them. Prior to offering concessions, the U.S. must decide what concessions in which sectors to put on the table. The domestic decision-making process is not easy or straightforward. It involves attempting to define a "national economic interest," at best an amalgam of a variety of social and political values.

The changing nature of the U.S. competitive posture in world markets has added to the controversy over the trade-liberalizing process. The significance of the issues for the United States is illustrated by a review of the dramatic changes in the U.S. world trading position in the post–World War II years.

Following World War II there was consensus in favor of economic intervention to support reconstruction of Europe and Japan. This meant necessarily more trade. The amount of trade among nations increased sharply as reconstruction efforts took hold. Between 1950 and 1970 world exports grew in value from $60 billion to roughly $300 billion.[1] In addition to trade in goods, reconstruction meant the transfer of technologies and infusion of capital. As a result, a "vast international capital market ... developed within which funds flow easily, rapidly, and in tremendous growing volume. The ease of communications has broken down international boundaries to the flow of ideas and information."[2]

The United States accepted the leadership role in redefining

---

[1]Organization for Economic Cooperation and Development, *Policy Perspective for International Trade and Economic Relations,* Report by the High-Level Group on Trade and Related Problems (Paris, 1972), p. 17 (hereafter cited as Rey group, for its chairman, Jean Rey).

[2]Commission on International Trade and Investment Policy, *United States International Economic Policy in an Interdependent World,* Report to the President (Washington, D.C., July 1971), p. 6 (hereafter cited as Williams Commission).

the world's economic relations: "[The] radical change in international economic relations was orginally based very largely on the resolve and generosity of the United States. Given the position in which the European countries and Japan found themselves in 1945, economic co-operation with the United States was bound to be a one-sided affair." Between 1945 and 1955 the United States transferred a total of $33.5 billion to Western Europe. Between 1945 and 1952 Japan received more than $2 billion.[3] The United States also aided recovery by allowing unequal application of trade gains. U.S. trading partners maintained quantitative restrictions against U.S. goods, thus encouraging domestic production. The United States financed reconstruction activities by sustaining a continuous balance of payments deficit.

In Europe the formation and expansion of the European Economic Community and the formation of the European Free Trade Association contributed to further recovery and growth. During the decade 1960–70, intra-Community trade quadrupled. European prosperity encouraged growth in trade with nonmember countries as well; nonmember imports grew by 130 percent in the same decade.[4]

Japan's economic growth in the twenty years from 1950 to 1970 constituted an "unprecedented performance." The economy grew at a rate better than 10 percent per year in real terms. Japan's growth has been largely outwardly directed. In 1960, Japan's exports accounted for 3.6 percent of total world exports; by 1969 the figure stood at 6.6 percent. During the 1960s the growth rate of Japanese exports approached 19 percent a year, approximately twice as fast as the growth of total world exports.[5]

While the United States benefited from the economic recovery of Europe and Japan, the country also began to feel the effects of

---

[3]Rey group, p. 23, inclusive of quotation.
[4]Williams Commission, pp. 202–3.
[5]Ibid., pp. 214–15.

competition. The formation of the EC had a negative side in that nonmember countries faced trade disadvantages.

In 1966 the European Community promulgated the centerpiece of its Common Agricultural Policy—grains regulations—and the result for U.S. agriculture was dramatic. In the decade 1960–70, the United States had competed successfully for its share of growing Community trade in industrial goods, but agricultural trade with the Community was less vigorous. "The member states' total agricultural imports almost doubled during the decade, but imports from nonmembers increased by only about one-third. There was virtually no increase after 1964. Agricultural imports from the United States actually declined by $300 million between 1966 and 1969."[6]

The amount of trade subject to import restriction or to preferential trading arrangements, such as special trade agreements between colonial powers and their former colonies, posed growing difficulties. The European Community maintained restrictions on industrial items of interest to Japan, which then sought a larger market in the United States. Japan maintained restrictions on items of interest to the other industrialized countries. The U.S. placed restrictions on cotton textiles, ceramic tile, stainless steel flatware, steel mill products and petroleum products.

The full extent of trade restrictions was not initially recognized. Restrictions not subject to rules of the General Agreement on Tariffs and Trade [GATT][7] were being negotiated on a bilateral basis between the exporting and the importing country. These "voluntary" restrictions were discussed against the background of a threat of mandatory import quotas.

Because U.S. "voluntary" restraints are negotiated by the government, their existence is known. In other countries, they are negotiated industry to industry[8] or company to company, and

---

[6]Ibid., p. 203.

[7]The General Agreement on Tariffs and Trade, known as GATT, is both an international agreement setting forth trade rules and a secretariat overseeing those rules.

[8]The distinction between government and industry becomes blurred when the industry is partly nationalized.

may not be widely known. "These arrangements often are not publicized, and the scope of the problem is therefore not fully known. Yet trade flows are affected by this network of barriers and the matter is one of concern to the whole trading community."[9]

From 1964 to 1969, the United States trade balance deteriorated by $5 billion, although it was still in surplus. Inflation "induced by accelerated government expenditures, including those accompanying the war in Vietnam, without timely and commensurate increase in taxation,"[10] attracted large amounts of imports. The trade balance did go into deficit in 1971 by $2 billion. The United States has, by and large, continued to show deficits of ever greater amounts. In 1983 the United States trade deficit was $67 billion; in 1984, $114 billion; in 1985, $124 billion.[11]

The loss of U.S. preeminence in world trade changed the trade debate in some sectors of production from support of freer trade to a call for fair trade. The number of "escape clause" petitions and unfair trade cases increased. The U.S. government negotiated "voluntary" export restraints with major U.S. suppliers of such goods as color television sets and nonrubber footwear. For the steel industry, suffering from sluggish demand in a recession economy and from competition from lower-priced imports, the government in 1977 devised a "trigger price mechanism" whereby steel imported at a price lower than that of Japan (considered to be the most efficient producer) automatically triggered a dumping or unfair trade practice investigation.

The U.S. also sought greater competitive opportunities through revisions in its role in monetary arrangements. Pressure on the dollar resulted from its central role in the world's econ-

---

[9]Williams Commission, p. 87.

[10]Ibid., p. 4.

[11]Merchandise trade balance on a balance of payments basis, one of several ways to calculate the trade deficit. Another commonly used method, known as C.I.F., for cost, insurance and freight, yields trade deficit figures of $70 billion for 1983, $123 billion for 1984, and $148.5 billion for 1985.

omy and a fixed exchange rate. This was compounded by a continuing balance of payments deficit; the harmonization of tax practices among the members of the European Community leading to further dampening of imports and the expansion of the European Community; and growing import competition in general. To meet these problems, the United States sought "substantial exchange rate realignment"[12] and changes in the world's trading system. Both of these objectives were advanced in August 1971 "when President Nixon shook America's trading partners by suspending the convertibility of the dollar and imposing a ten percent surcharge on imports."[13] For exchange rates, these actions led to abandonment of the Bretton Woods system of fixed exchange rates to a system of floating exchange rates. On trade, countries moved closer to the decision to launch a new round of multilateral trade negotiations.

The Tokyo Round was negotiated in this foreign and domestic economic climate. Despite these adverse conditions, an agreement was achieved. While the results were less than had been hoped or expected at the outset, the conclusion was, nevertheless, better than a "mini-harvest."

In the Senate, the legislation implementing the negotiated results, the Trade Agreements Act of 1979, was passed with only four negative votes. Only seven members of the House of Representatives voted against it. By the time the bill came to a floor vote, a battle was not anticipated. Floor debate was desultory; press reporting was limited. In the months leading up to this final congressional action, a coming battle had been depicted that would make other difficult legislative efforts, such as the 1978 energy legislation, look easy. The battle did not materialize. Why?

Undoubtedly, there were several keys to the success. A precedent had been set in the Kennedy Round and lessons learned

---

[12]I.M. Destler, *Making Foreign Economic Policy* (Brookings Institution, 1980), p. 139.
[13]Ibid.

from it.[14] A strong international structure existed in which the United States had long been a leader. Despite the intricacies of trade, the world community has on many occasions been able to reach agreement on these issues, while other noneconomic issues, including those affecting war and peace, were in deadlock. Part of the key lies in the existence of GATT.

The multilateral trading system was established in 1947 with the acceptance by twenty-three countries of the General Agreement on Tariffs and Trade, a negotiated international agreement specifying trading rules to which the Contracting Parties pledged to adhere. It was expected at the time that an International Trade Organization would be established to serve as the institutional body overseeing the provisions of the agreement, but the ITO did not come into existence and GATT has since evolved into a secretariat. (The United States acceded to the General Agreement on Tariffs and Trade by executive order; Congress routinely noted its nonrecognition of GATT until the passage of the Trade Act of 1974, when Congress directed the Executive to seek certain changes in the international organization, and explicitly authorized expenditures relating to GATT.)[15]

The cornerstones of GATT are the principles of nondiscrimination and equal treatment of imported and domestic goods once customs duties have been paid. Nondiscrimination is applied through the most-favored-nation (MFN) provision whereby a concession granted to one party is extended to all other parties.[16] Similarly, protective actions are to be taken on an

---

[14]The Kennedy Round of trade negotiations, named for the late President John F. Kennedy, immediately preceded the Tokyo Round. It took place between 1964 and 1967. It was successful in accomplishing a reduction in industrial tariff rates to a neglible level.

[15]See Alan William Wolff, "The U.S. Mandate for Trade Negotiations," *Virginia Journal of International Law* 16 (Spring 1976):505–64. See especially p. 524.

[16]The most-favored-nation *provision* in the GATT allows for most-favored-nation *treatment*, which is the extension to any eligible third party of the agreements negotiated directly with any other party. For example, if the U.S. negotiates with country A the reduction of tariffs on clothespins, eligible country B's clothespin exports will also benefit from that reduction. The U.S. automatically extends MFN treatment to its trading

MFN basis; that is, the protection is taken temporarily against a *product,* not against a particular country's product.

This multilateral system for the conduct of the world's commerce replaced the practice of bilateral negotiation and unilateral abrogation of the 1930s. Through this system, world industrial tariffs were reduced to an average of 8 to 10 percent following the implementation of the Kennedy Round tariff cuts agreed to in 1967. In contrast, the U.S. tariff rate in 1933 had stood at some 54 percent following passage of the Smoot-Hawley Tariff Act in 1930.

If an existing and relatively well-accepted international body was the key to making the international aspect succeed, the American domestic key lay in the degree to which negotiators were able to bring Congress and key elements of the American private sector along during the process of negotiation. This had not been achieved in SALT, the Panama Canal, or the Law of the Sea.

---

partners, unless they are specifically excluded by law. See United States Trade Representative, *A Preface to Trade,* 1982.

2

Preparing for the Tokyo Round

THE DECISION TO INAUGURATE the Tokyo Round of trade talks was not a hasty one. Discussion about a new round and what it should and could entail had been underway since the Kennedy Round of trade negotiations ended in 1967.[1] Indeed from the standpoint of trade negotiators, negotiating is not an event, it is a process. The process, generally speaking, has three phases: preparing for a round, being involved in a round, and implementing the results of a round.

The Kennedy Round had succeeded in reducing average world tariff rates on industrial goods to a negligible level. It had also introduced a system of industrial tariff reduction by formula, rather than by negotiating on an item-by-item basis. These were major accomplishments. On agriculture, the round accomplished little; the United States was most interested in gaining a foothold in the European Community, but the EC's Common Agricultural Policy, buttressed by a system of variable levies, proved nonnegotiable. Although U.S. negotiators insisted that

---

[1]In his "Sources of Instability in the World Trading System," Harald B. Malmgren writes, "The process itself of establishing a new consensus domestically and internationally took roughly seven years." *Journal of International Affairs* 30 (Spring/Summer 1976), p. 9.

U.S. agriculture had gained as a result of the round,[2] agricultural interests claimed they had been sold down the river.

Kennedy Round negotiators had also reached agreement on the dismantling of two nontariff barriers to trade maintained by the United States. One, called the American Selling Price, was a method of customs valuation applied primarily to benzenoid chemicals. ASP set the price of the import for customs purposes as that of its domestic competitor. The antidumping measure, the other agreed to by U.S. negotiators, was designed to bring the U.S. law into conformance with GATT rules. Neither of these measures went into effect: in the first instance, because of lack of action by the Congress to implement ASP; and because of action, in the second instance, to override the executive agreement. The failure of the Congress to agree to what the U.S. Executive had negotiated was a major concern to U.S. trading partners. It was also a major concern to U.S. trade negotiators, who wondered how they could negotiate credibly in the face of possible override action by Congress. This experience in the Kennedy Round led executive branch officials and legislators to consider how better to manage the U.S. political process to avoid similar results in future negotiations.

The substantive agenda for what became the Tokyo Round of trade negotiations included the further reduction of tariffs on industrial and agricultural goods; nontariff barriers; the role of the developing countries; and subsidies and countervailing duties. It grew out of existing economic conditions and the efforts of the Kennedy Round. The growing use of nontariff barriers to trade concerned governments. NTBs are wide-ranging and fall into a number of categories. Government aid to industry, for instance, constitutes a subsidy and is trade distortional when the subsidized industry's exports compete with nonsubsidized products. Some NTBs such as "buy national" laws are expressly

---

[2]See the testimony of John A. Schnittker, Under Secretary of Agriculture in "The Future of U.S. Foreign Trade Policy," Hearings before the Subcommittee on Foreign Economic Policy, pp. 29–39. Joint Economic Committee, Congress of the United States, 90th Congress, 1st session, July 11, 1967.

discriminatory. Others consist of rules applied in a discriminatory fashion. "They are diverse, complicated, embedded in legislation, and are frequently designed to achieve social objectives unrelated to international trade."[3] They are difficult to identify, difficult to evaluate with respect to their impact on trade, and difficult to negotiate.

The industrialized countries were also aware of the importance of the less developed countries (LDCs) to the well-being of the world's economy. During the late 1960s and early 1970s there was great optimism about the role of increased trade in the development process. A system of generalized preferences for LDC exports had been agreed to. European countries established special trade relationships with those developing countries with whom they had had a colonial relationship, an arrangement that brought mutual benefit. These arrangements, however, also brought concern in that an increasing portion of world trade was being conducted outside the GATT framework. Members of the OECD were anxious to bring developing countries into the multilateral framework while recognizing that they would require certain derogations from GATT rules.

For the United States, liberalization of trade in agricultural products remained an important holdover from the Kennedy Round. In addition to protecting the extensive market of Europe, the Common Agricultural Policy leads to displacement of competitors' exports to third countries because of the practice of subsidizing. The CAP is supported by a system of variable levies applied to a particular product. A variable levy is an import duty equalling the difference between the EC's target price for domestically produced goods and the lowest available market price for imports. The system of variable levies, then, supports the very high target price for the products of European farmers, which in turn produces a return sufficiently high to keep farmers farming. Thus the regional goal of European self-sufficiency in food is achieved. Because of the high target prices, farmers tend to

---

[3]Williams Commission, p. 74.

produce more than can be absorbed in the European market. This excess is disposed of on the world market at artificially low prices achieved through export subsidies. The United States wanted to curb the use of export subsidies and gain greater access to the European market. The United States also wanted trade concessions to compensate for an expanding European Community.

Leaders of U.S. industry, too, had concerns they hoped would be addressed during the course of the Tokyo Round. During the 1970s, business complaints about import competition and unfair trade practices grew. Business leaders sought redress through petitioning the appropriate administrative agency. In 1975 the International Trade Commission instituted thirteen investigations of escape clause petitions. The Treasury Department initiated thirty-eight countervailing duty investigations, a record number.[4] While the increase in petitioning certainly reflected increased competition from imports, both fair and unfair, it was directly related to changes in U.S. laws making the opportunity to seek relief from the government a more viable option for U.S. business. The requirement for relief from fair, but disruptive, import competition was changed from the necessity that import competition be a "major" cause of injury to a "substantial" one. The process of investigating unfair trade cases was expedited.

Preparing for a round of trade negotiations involved talks with other governments. By the time the Tokyo Round of Multilateral Trade Negotiations officially opened in September 1973, these issues and problems had been discussed within and among governments. In the early 1960s the Organization for Economic Cooperation and Development[5] had held discussions on restrictive government procurement policies. In November 1967 the GATT annual session agreed that "a new comprehensive pro-

---

[4]*International Economic Report of the President* (Washington, D.C.: Government Printing Office, 1976), p. 44.

[5]See glossary of terms. The OECD is an organization made up of the developed nations and is a forum in which these countries discuss international economic matters.

gram of preparatory work for a further round of trade negotiations should be initiated."[6] From 1968 through 1970, experts from the Contracting Parties to the GATT met in Geneva to catalogue existing nontariff barriers to trade, voice complaints against their use, and draft some codes of conduct.[7]

In the United States, part of the preparations for a new round involved developing a "national consensus" on U.S. trade and economic policy. The appointment of a presidential commission to study the issues and make recommendations is a method often used by administrations to garner support for a policy initiative. On May 21, 1970, President Nixon appointed the Commission on International Trade and Investment Policy (known as the Williams Commission) to "study the principal problems, . . . assess U.S. policies, and produce a set of policy recommendations for the 1970s which would take full account of the changes that have taken place on the world economic scene since the end of World War II."[8] In its final report, the commission urged that "no time . . . be lost in getting these negotiations underway." The commission targeted nontariff barriers, agriculture, export subsidies, and tariffs among other issues for negotiation. The negotiations, the commission said, "should be launched at the highest political level through a joint initiative by the United States, Western Europe, Canada and Japan." The United States should seek reciprocity conceived in terms of the entire negotiation. The commission also noted the role of Congress and the private sector:

More than ever before, the negotiations—and the preparations therefore—must involve the private sector and the Congress so as to ensure domestic consensus on U.S. objectives. Key congres-

---

[6]General Agreement on Tariffs and Trade, *The Tokyo Round of Multilateral Trade Negotiations,* Report of the Director-General of GATT (Geneva, April 1979), p. 2.

[7]See *Tokyo Round,* Report of the Director-General, p. 2; Senate Finance Committee Report, Trade Agreements Act of 1979, p. 2; Alan Wm. Wolff, "The Larger Political and Economic Role of the Tokyo Round," *Law and Policy in International Business* 12 (1980): 1–19. See especially pp. 2–4.

[8]See Williams Commission, letter of transmittal of Report to the President.

sional committees should be consulted at an early stage and kept informed of subsequent developments. Some members of Congress and key representatives of the private sector, where appropriate, should be included in the U.S. delegations, as members or consultants. Arrangements should be made for periodic consultations with business, farm, labor and consumer groups.[9]

The Williams Commission also urged that a study of the issues be undertaken in the OECD.[10] This suggestion was taken up at the OECD Ministerial level meeting in June 1971 and culminated in the report *Policy Perspectives for International Trade and Economic Relations,* Report by the High-Level Group on Trade and Related Problems [the Rey group], issued in August 1972. The group supported continuation of efforts for further trade liberalization but warned that "liberalisation becomes more difficult the further it proceeds, especially in those branches of economic activity where it has always met serious obstacles." The group also voiced the prevailing view concerning the political necessity of continued trade negotiations: "A new effort to secure greater liberalisation, achieved through negotiation, is needed not only for the direct benefits it will bring but because without it the divisive forces of protectionism will grow stronger, with the risk that the world will slip back into an era of restriction and ultimately of contraction of the international economic system."[11]

Where the OECD group and the Williams Commission strongly disagreed was on the subject of trade in agricultural goods. The Williams Commission was forthright in calling for the significant opening of trade in agriculture with the European Community. That meant opening the Common Agricultural

---

[9]Williams Commission, pp. 300–307.

[10]This had been suggested by Senator Abraham Ribicoff. "Senator Ribicoff's call for creation of a 'wise men's group' was heard, albeit after some resistance by the executive branch in Washington, and the Rey group, named after its chairman, Jean Rey, got underway in Paris." See Malmgren, "Sources of Instability," p. 11.

[11]OECD, Rey group, p. 110.

Policy to negotiation, a goal the commission urged, terming the CAP "protectionist." In its section on agriculture, the OECD group spoke generally of countries' domestic agricultural policies, thus including the various price support systems of the United States, and did not mention the CAP in particular. These differences were to continue into the trade negotiation itself.

In the executive branch, responsibility for preparing for and directing U.S. participation in the Tokyo Round was held by the Office of the Special Trade Representative [STR]. The job of Special Trade Representative, whose title was changed in the Trade Agreements Act of 1979 to United States Trade Representative, was established by President John Kennedy in 1962 at the urging of Representative Wilbur Mills, who was then chairman of the House Ways and Means Committee. The office, situated in the Executive Office of the President, replaced the State Department as the lead agency for trade policy formulation and negotiations. Creation of the function and office of STR consolidated trade policy responsibilities which had been scattered among several departments and interdepartmental committees.[12] But the major goal of the proponents of the STR was to remove trade negotiations from the State Department, which, it was argued, sacrificed U.S. commercial needs for foreign policy purposes. In the Trade Act of 1974 Congress strengthened the office by establishing it by statute, and compensating the STR at the level of a cabinet officer; congressional pressure had resulted earlier in the Nixon administration's abandonment of a

---

[12]*Trade Agreements Committee:* This committee was responsible for information regarding initiation and implementation of negotiations. The State Department representative served as the chair; the other departments and agencies represented were Agriculture, Commerce, Defense, Interior, Labor, Treasury, the International Cooperation Administration (no longer in existence) and the Tariff Commission (now the International Trade Commission).

Committee for Reciprocity Information: Same membership as TAC. The Tariff Commission representative served as chair. The committee solicited views of interested groups and individuals as to trade concessions the U.S. might make.

Trade Policy Committee: Established at cabinet level to advise and assist the president on administration of the trade agreements program. The secretary of commerce served as its chair. It reviewed recommendations of the TAC.

plan to merge STR with that administration's creation, the Council on International Economic Policy.[13] In its report on the 1974 trade legislation, the House Ways and Means Committee noted that

> . . . a strong and independent office, headed by a government official reporting directly to the President *and responsible to the Congress,* is the best means of assuring that in trade policy matters the United States is speaking with one voice on behalf of the executive branch and that positions taken accurately reflect the intent of the Congress.[14]

Placing STR in the Office of the President and keeping the office intentionally small served the function of keeping STR without a constituency. The purpose of the departments of Agriculture, Commerce, Labor, and to some extent Treasury and State—the departments mainly concerned with trade policy—is to represent the views of those comprising their constituencies. (Needless to say, those departments must reconcile and synthesize the wide-ranging views of those making up their constituent groups.) STR's purpose on the other hand was to develop a national policy that necessarily spanned and synthesized a wider range of concerns.

The STR in its design and as it was configured during the Tokyo Round negotiation was a small office with a reputation of having highly qualified and interested staff. Staffing patterns were basically stable and those changes that did occur were often a result of cross-fertilization among trade offices in other agencies and to and from the Hill.

Trade policy positions and negotiating instructions were developed by means of an interagency process functioning at three levels and chaired at each level by the STR's office. The Trade Policy Staff Committee was the first level and was composed of senior-level civil servants. The Trade Policy Review Group at the

---

[13]Destler, *Making Foreign Economic Policy,* pp. 129–54.
[14]Wolff, "U.S. Mandate for Trade," pp. 551–52. Emphasis added by Wolff.

assistant secretary level reviewed issues that could not be resolved at the TPSC level. And finally the Trade Policy Committee met at the cabinet level of government. The department most interested in the issue under consideration drafted a policy paper for discussion. During the period 1977–79, most issues were resolved at the TPRG level.

The final push and conclusion of the Tokyo Round came about during the Carter administration. Carter's special trade representative was Robert Strauss, a well-known politician with many friends and associates on Capitol Hill and in the private sector. Strauss' two top deputies were Alonzo L. McDonald and Alan William Wolff. McDonald was brought in from the private sector and assumed the position of head of delegation in Geneva. He managed the conduct of the negotiation and developed a lobbying strategy for selling the results to Congress. Wolff was a career civil servant and lawyer and a specialist in international trade. He was in charge of the policy formulation process in Washington and chaired the TPRG. Wolff had served other administrations in the STR's office. In 1974 and 1975 he was general counsel at STR, having served previously as deputy general counsel in 1973. He was instrumental in drafting the legislation that became the U.S. authority to enter the Tokyo Round (the Trade Act of 1974) and in negotiating with Congress the changes in that bill. For six months in 1975 Wolff was acting head of delegation in Geneva.

Following the issuance of the Williams Commission report, but preceding that of the OECD group, President Nixon took some actions that led to fundamental changes in trade and monetary arrangements and that helped move forward resolve to open a new round of trade negotiations. The "Nixon shocks" of August 1971 were followed in February 1972 by the issuance of two "Declarations on International Economic Relations," one between the United States and the European Community, and one between the United States and Japan. In March of that year, the GATT Council met and agreed to the principle of initiating a new trade round in 1973 under the auspices of GATT, a decision that was endorsed at the GATT annual session in November 1972. During the first half of 1973 a preparatory committee met to work out what the negotiations might entail. In September 1973 at a ministerial meeting held in Tokyo, the Tokyo Declaration, announcing a new round of multilateral trade negotiations, was issued on behalf of 102 countries,[15] more than had ever participated in a trade negotiation. The declaration stated a goal of concluding the round by the end of 1975; as it happened, the results of the Tokyo Round were not initialed until April 1979.

Part of the reason for the delay in concluding the negotiation was the delay in the start-up of the negotiation. An initial two-year delay was due to the fact that the United States did not have authority to negotiate in hand until January 1975. By then, there was hesitation about going forward in the face of an upcoming U.S. presidential election. Additionally, the negotiations themselves were stalled over the issue of agricultural trade and where and how those negotiations were to take place.

The pace and substance of the negotiation were also shaped by the international economic and political climate. The problems that the Tokyo Round set out to cope with were not new; specific issues and the conditions giving rise to those issues had been documented during the 1960s. "Voluntary" export restraints had been employed in the sixties. The "short-term" agreement on cotton textiles, which evolved into the "long-term" agreement and then into the multi-fiber agreement, was first negotiated in 1961. Concerns about growing protectionism were not new. "Stemming the tide" of protectionist sentiment is a well-worn phrase and justification for the initiation of trade talks.

Nevertheless, the worldwide recession touched off by the OPEC oil embargo of 1973 and the subsequent hike in the price of oil certainly increased the difficulty of trade-liberalizing efforts. Growing trade deficits in the United States increased pressures for protection. Difficult economic conditions—growing unemployment and higher prices—heightened expressions

---

[15]*Tokyo Round,* Report of the Director-General, pp. 4–8.

of opposition to import competition and the internationalization of capital.

Organized labor in the late 1960s began to voice opposition to government policies to facilitate free trade and foreign investment. Labor economists warned of technology transfers, investment outflows, the displacement of workers and permanent loss of jobs. The rise of the multinational corporation, they said, made obsolete "eighteenth and nineteenth century theories of free competition and comparative advantage."[16] I.W. Abel and Floyd E. Smith, labor leaders who sat on the Williams Commission, so disagreed with the commission's report and recommendations that they wrote a minority statement, saying in part: "The strategy and recommendations will make the United States a third-rate industrial power—with the continuing displacement of U.S. production, including high-technology products.... We do not believe, as the Report implies, that America must choose between free trade and protectionism in the 1970s, because international business and banking operations make such theories out of date."[17] Organized labor had been an enthusiastic supporter of the Trade Expansion Act of 1962 which authorized U.S. participation in the Kennedy Round negotiations. By 1970 the AFL–CIO was supporting mandatory import quota legislation and opposing legislation to authorize the United States to participate in future trade negotiations.

Industries seeking import relief throughout the decade were varied, and included producers of nonrubber footwear, stainless steel flatware, television sets and parts, shrimp, nuts, bolts and screws, honey, and iron blue pigments.[18] In 1977 the International Trade Commission investigated petitions for import relief

---

[16]See "A Labor View of Foreign Investment and Trade Issues," by Nat Goldfinger, in *Compendium of Papers: Volume 1, Papers submitted to the Commission on International Trade and Investment Policy* and published in conjunction with the commission's Report to the President, July 1971, pp. 913–28. Quoted material, page 920.

[17]Williams Commission, pp. 338–39. Abel was the president of the United Steelworkers of America; and Smith was the international president of the International Association of Machinists and Aerospace Workers.

[18]*International Economic Report of the President,* 1977, p. 47.

from more than twenty industries with a trade coverage of almost $5 billion. The commission recommended relief be granted on $3 billion worth of trade.[19] Orderly Marketing Agreements negotiated with the primary exporting country were entered into with more frequency; OMAs were negotiated for specialty steel, color television sets and nonrubber footwear.

Increased pressures for protectionism from industries in the United States reflected poor economic conditions worldwide. In 1977 trade volume expanded only 4 percent. The United States was joined by other countries of the world in imposing new restrictions on trade; the GATT secretariat estimated that new restrictive trade measures were imposed on 3 to 5 percent of world trade in the period 1974–77.[20]

The steel industry presented a particularly difficult problem. Sluggish recovery from the 1974 recession led to excess steel capacity worldwide. Over the five-year period 1972–77, the cost of production of steel in the United States rose by 89 percent.

> Poor domestic sales, reflecting sluggish demand and an increase in the import share, led to a drop in steel production in 1977. This development and other factors led to a series of layoffs and plant closings in 1977. These were concentrated in older steel plants in Ohio, Pennsylvania, and New York. This pattern was dictated by the desire of domestic firms to consolidate their operations in their most efficient installations. The timing and allocation of the layoffs were also affected by provisions in the new labor contract that will increase the cost of layoffs after 1977. The cost of meeting environmental standards at older facilities also played an important role. Thus, the layoffs reflected efforts by the industry to reduce costs over the long term, as well as to respond to the immediate problem of weak demand and import competition. Although several factors contributed to the layoffs, public attention focused on the problem of imports.[21]

---

[19]*Economic Report of the President,* January 1978, p. 134.

[20]Ibid., p. 133.

[21]Ibid., p. 136.

The steel industry, alleging the sale of imported steel at less than fair value, filed a number of dumping charges. The Carter administration responded by developing a "trigger price" system, whereby imports that entered the country at a price lower than that of the most efficient producer (considered to be Japan) automatically triggered a dumping investigation. Although this system was labeled "protectionist" by some, the administration contended that the system was in fact more palatable than other options such as tariffs or quotas.[22]

Liberal or free trade arguments are often made in the name of the general public, the theory being that the public at large benefits from freer trade, even though "special interests" may suffer temporarily in the period of adjustment. There is however no organization that represents the general public or consumers, and it is difficult moreover to find a member of the "public" who is not also a member of a "special interest." Those organizations such as the League of Women Voters that do seek to speak for the general interest, which they believe is supported by pursuit of liberal trade policies, often find that their voices are weak compared to those of injured industry and displaced workers.

Despite a climate that had worsened over the years of preparing to make the decision to open another round of international trade negotiations, the stage was set to move forward. Before the United States could proceed, suitable understandings had to be reached with two indispensable elements: the Congress and the private sector.

---

[22]Ibid., pp. 136–37.

3

Congressional Consideration: The Trade Act of 1974

I N THE MAKING OF TRADE POLICY, which is a foreign economic policy, the Constitution places with Congress the authority to "lay and collect Taxes, Duties (and) Imposts" and to "regulate Commerce with foreign Nations."[1] The Executive is given sole responsibility to negotiate with foreign nations. Since a negotiation without implementation is pointless, Congress and the Executive must work together prior to negotiating with foreign governments to determine acceptable limits and approaches. Since 1934, Congress has delegated limited authority to the Executive to negotiate the reduction of tariffs. Because tariffs are quantitative, Congress has been able to control trade concessions by specifying the percentage range of tariff reduction the Executive may offer in its negotiations. Once negotiated, tariff cuts become effective with no further action on the part of the Congress.

The congressional committees with primary jurisdiction over trade matters are the House Committee on Ways and Means and the Senate Finance Committee. The House Subcommittee on

---

[1]U.S. Constitution, Article I, Section 8.

Trade, then chaired by Representative Charles Vanik (D-OH), had responsibility for overseeing the progress of the Tokyo Round and considering its results. The Senate Finance Committee was chaired by Senator Russell Long (D-LA), who exerted considerable influence over matters of particular interest to the committee; for instance, the Finance Committee was very interested in agricultural trade, in part because of the orientation of Long and other senators from agricultural states. Senator Long had great influence on the timing of committee action on legislation affecting the progress and results of the Tokyo Round. While Long set the political direction of the committee, the substance of trade matters was managed by the Subcommittee on International Trade chaired by Senator Abraham Ribicoff (D-CT).

The Special Trade Representative's office under Robert Strauss tended to work more closely with the Senate than with the House. The Senate was also the body to which interests such as the steel industry turned in their attempts to tighten administrative procedures for various trade laws and regulations. The Finance Committee enjoys a reputation of being more protectionist than the Ways and Means Committee.

Authority for the United States to enter the Tokyo Round was provided by the Trade Act of 1974. Passage of this act had been preceded by legislative attempts in 1968-71 to impose sweeping import quotas and to authorize other restrictive trade measures. The Trade Act of 1974 was at the time the most comprehensive trade legislation passed by Congress and provided for the strongest congressional role ever. The act also gave the Executive more substantive and procedural guidance than had previous trade negotiating mandates.

The genesis of the Trade Act of 1974 has been well analyzed in published accounts, principally by I.M. Destler in his book *Making Foreign Economic Policy* and by Robert A. Pastor in *Congress and the Politics of U.S. Foreign Economic Policy.* Alan Wolff has also written on certain aspects of the trade negotiating authority.[2] Administration drafting of a bill and congressional consideration and redrafting were influenced by a myriad of factors: intra-executive rivalries; reform of the committee system and the retirement of Wilbur Mills, chairman of the House Ways and Means Committee; the OPEC oil embargo; the Watergate scandal; Henry Kissinger's interest in obtaining most-favored-nation status for the USSR and the opposition to that goal by those concerned with freedom of emigration from the Soviet Union; private sector concern that its views be heard; and congressional interest in maintaining an active role during the period of negotiation and with respect to the implementation of the results of the negotiation. The broader backdrop to the legislation was the changing nature of the U.S. role in the world economy, and the perceived need, endorsed by the administration's own study commission, to insist that the European Community and Japan take a lead in assuming responsibilities commensurate with their economic strength and vitality.

The Trade Act of 1974 did more than provide the Executive with authority to participate in multilateral trade negotiations. It also helped make invoking the escape clause, that is, petitioning for relief from imports, a more viable option by lessening the extent of injury imports must cause before relief may be granted. The act strengthened the adjustment assistance program (the Williams Commission's preferred import relief alternative), which provided assistance to workers for retraining and relocating, to companies for retooling, and to affected communities for economic recovery. Like escape clause proceedings, the adjustment assistance program had been criticized for the rigidity of its injury requirement, leading in the period between the Trade Expansion Act of 1962 and the Trade Act of 1974 to very few affirmative findings. Congress also gave itself more control over escape clause proceedings by stipulating that it could by concurrent resolution override the president if he chose

---

[2] Destler, *Making Foreign Economic Policy;* Robert A. Pastor, *Congress and the Politics of U.S. Foreign Economic Policy* (Berkeley: University of California Press, 1980); Wolff, "The U.S. Mandate for Trade Negotiations."

not to act on an affirmative determination of relief by the International Trade Commission.[3]

A provision of the Trade Act that was to receive attention during the course of the MTN was the waiver of the counter-vailing duty (CVD) law. The CVD law provided that the United States could impose duties on imported goods that were deter-mined to have been subsidized by the exporting country. The U.S. had no injury test as part of its law—duties could be imposed even if no harm to domestic industry were caused. The use of export subsidies and the addition of an injury test to U.S. law were on the agenda for the MTN. U.S. trading partners—the European Community in particular—would not negotiate on export subsidies if their goods were subject to countervailing. The administration thus sought and Congress granted the ability to waive the collection of countervailing duties for four years after the passage of the Trade Act under specified conditions.

The most controversial "traditional" foreign policy issue em-bodied in the Trade Act of 1974 was the proposed granting of most-favored-nation status to the Soviet Union. This was an item favored by Henry Kissinger. The proposal was met in Congress by a counterproposal, the Jackson-Vanik amendment, tying MFN status for the USSR to its emigration policies. This amendment resulted in threats of veto of the whole bill and delays in congressional consideration of the legislation. From the standpoint of trade policy and the MTN, it was essentially a side issue.[4]

The provisions of the Trade Act of 1974 that earned it ap-praisal as a "unique constitutional experiment"[5] were those

---

[3]The International Trade Commission (before the 1974 trade legislation it was the Tariff Commission) is the body that investigates petitions for relief from import competition (i.e., escape clause petitions) and recommends action to the president. The commission can find in the negative, in the positive, or be divided. If the commission finds in the positive, it recommends a form of relief to the president. The president must decide whether to accept the ITC recommendation. The president may decide to provide a form of relief other than that recommended by the ITC. The override provision gives Congress leverage over the presidential decision-making process.

[4]See Destler's account in *Making Foreign Economic Policy*.

[5]U.S. Senate, Committee on Finance, *Trade Agreements Act of 1979*, 17 July 1979.

guiding the involvement of Congress during the period of negotiation and the method of congressional approval of the results of negotiation. Congress also gave guidance on the substance of negotiating objectives for the MTN. Finally, Congress responded to complaints voiced by business leaders that during the Kennedy Round private sector advice was not adequately factored into the negotiation.

Negotiating Authority: Congressional Review of MTN Results

In order for the Executive to negotiate credibly with other countries, those countries must have confidence that the results of the negotiation will be accepted by the Congress. Tariff negotiations are possible because Congress specifies a percentage range of allowable reduction. For the Tokyo Round, for instance, Congress authorized the Executive to eliminate tariffs of 5 percent or less and to reduce most other tariffs by as much as 60 percent. That type of negotiating authority is not possible for nontariff barriers, and yet authority is needed. During the Kennedy Round, moreover, the Executive had negotiated on two U.S. nontariff barriers, only to have the results repudiated by Congress. U.S. trading partners would not negotiate seriously with the United States without some reasonable assurance of congressional acceptance of negotiated agreements. To meet both political and constitutional requirements, the Executive had to negotiate at home before negotiating abroad.

In its initial draft, the Nixon administration had asked for advance authority to implement negotiated international agreements on various customs procedures.[6] For other NTB agreements, the executive asked for authority to implement unless one house of Congress vetoed the agreement within ninety days. This administration position represented a compromise of views, with

---

[6]Destler describes the evolution of the trade act beginning with its formulation within the Executive and its treatment by each house of Congress.

the State Department and the Council on International Economic Policy advocating that the administration request unlimited authority under the theory that international negotiations are the purview of the executive branch of government.[7]

The device recommended by the Nixon administration for congressional implementation of Tokyo Round agreements is known as the legislative veto. It has been used in a variety of statutes, sometimes for implementation purposes, e.g., for congressional "approval" of government reorganization plans proposed by the Executive and accepted by Congress unless vetoed, and sometimes for the purpose of providing a congressional "check" on executive actions. Congress for instance delegated to itself power to veto a presidential decision in escape clause cases. The device has been challenged throughout the years as unconstitutional, and indeed, in 1983, the Supreme Court found the legislative veto unconstitutional.

While the constitutionality issue was raised during House consideration of the Nixon bill, the basic veto procedure was not changed. The House bill did require that *all* NTB negotiation results be subject to a one-house veto.

The legislative veto procedure drew fire from the Senate Finance Committee and in particular from Senator Herman Talmadge, who argued that use of the veto for congressional acceptance or rejection of government reorganization schemes, on which the trade bill proposal was patterned, was an entirely different matter from use of a veto to make policy. Talmadge argued that "approval" of NTB negotiations via veto was unconstitutional and called for an affirmative vote of Congress in implementing such trade agreements. Talmadge's view prevailed in the Senate and in conference committee, where the House accepted the Senate version.

Executive concerns about an affirmative implementing vote by Congress were that negotiated results would languish in committee or be subject to "Christmas tree" amendments ad-

---

[7]Pastor, *Congress and the Politics of U.S. Foreign Economic Policy,* p. 142.

vanced by disaffected interests. To meet these concerns, Congress provided in the Trade Act of 1974 (section 105) for special legislative procedures:

1) Presidential notification of intent to enter trade agreements sent to Congress ninety days before entering. During that ninety-day period Congress could advise the Executive as to whether the Executive should seek renegotiation of any agreements.

2) Executive-legislative consultations during the ninety-day period, at the end of which time the Executive would submit a formal implementing bill to Congress.

3) Congressional consideration of about sixty days in each house. If either jurisdictional committee failed to report the bill to the floor an automatic discharge would go into effect.

4) Limited floor debate of twenty hours in each house. The bill was to be nonamendable and could not be recommitted.

These procedures were developed through consultations between the Executive and Senator Talmadge, who had initially insisted that any trade agreements be subject to the more usual legislative process.[8] They are known generally as "fast-track" procedures. Harald Malmgren, who was deputy special trade representative at the time, has described the search for a method of legislative consideration that would satisfy both executive and congressional concerns:

> The critical point in the informal, behind-the-scenes search for an acceptable compromise came in executive branch discussions with Senator Talmadge. He asked the Executive what the basic minimum requirement was for effective negotiation. The executive representatives explained that other governments wanted to know whether a deal was a deal in a short period of time—yes or no, up or down, without

---

[8]Richard S. Frank, "Trade Report/Distrust leads Congress to tie strings to new authority," *National Journal Reports* 6 (5 October 1974):1483–94.

alteration, within a few weeks of an ad referendum or informal agreement.... Senator Talmadge then suggested that the key seemed to lie in the need for a congressional vote, without the possibility of amendment of the package, within a specific, short period of time.... It was also suggested that in order for such a procedure to function properly it would be essential that the Executive and the Congress work very closely together prior to the approval of agreements by the negotiators, since automaticity of procedures could not by itself provide a total solution.[9]

Congress provided for congressional involvement during the period of negotiation itself by designating members from each house as official advisers to the negotiation. The special trade representative was to keep each adviser "currently informed on how the U.S. negotiating objectives are being met, the progress of the negotiations, and the nature of any changes in domestic law or the administration thereof which may be recommended to Congress to carry out any trade agreement."[10]

Being kept "currently informed" applied also to the staff of the Ways and Means and Finance committees. During the dormant period of the Tokyo Round, staff worked out agreements with the office of the STR about such matters as receipt of cables and whether they could be present in the negotiating rooms in Geneva. It was necessary for a formal agreement on the receipt of cables to be made because of the opposition of the State Department to the release of sensitive cables. The extent to which staff were allowed access to documents and the extent to which they were involved in the negotiating process was unusual: "[Direct participation in negotiating meetings] rarely has been done in the past, and in the case of trade negotiations, no example of congressional representatives being present in actual negotiations has been found, at least in the last four decades."[11]

Communication between congressional committees and STR

---

[9]Matthew J. Marks and Harald B. Malmgren, "Negotiating Nontariff Distortions to Trade," *Law and Policy in International Business* 7 (Spring 1975):339–40.

[10]U.S. Senate, Committee on Finance, *Trade Reform Act of 1974,* p. 113.

[11]Marks and Malmgren, "Negotiating Nontariff Distortions to Trade," pp. 337–38.

was good throughout preparations for and participation in the MTN. This was true of both the Nixon and Ford administrations (STR William Eberle and STR Frederick Dent) and the Carter administration (STR Strauss). A former Senate aide remembers that Strauss was somewhat more forthcoming with members and staff, largely because of Strauss's background and prior relationships. A former House staff aide remarked that Strauss was in closer contact with the Senate, and that Dent was more balanced in communicating with both the House and the Senate. Critics of Strauss say that he was too amenable, at least as far as accepting the views of Congress in the bill-writing phase.

During the last six months of the negotiation there was a congressional presence in Geneva. Staff from the Ways and Means Committee were present on a full-time basis. Finance Committee staff sent a team once a month for a week. The chairmen of the trade committees and subcommittees of the House and Senate travelled to Geneva at least once. Ambassador McDonald met with members in Washington about once a month.

Did members have an influence on the substance of the negotiation? Former Finance Committee Counsel Robert Cassidy says "yes," although it is "difficult to document." One reason for that difficulty is that during the negotiation members and staff avoided taking definitive positions on proposed U.S. policy. They did, however, make detailed comments. STR had guidance but not guarantees. Additionally, Cassidy has said,

> At times, the influence would be more implicit than explicit, in fact more often implicit. For example, congressional "influence" would occur when an interagency decision-making group anticipated some congressional problem and made their decision on what they thought Congress might do.... Based on their general day-to-day connections with Congress, it was rare for the administration to come up and say, "This is what we propose to do, what do you think about it?" That did happen, but it was fairly rare; an informal telephone conversation was much more the norm.[12]

---

[12]Interview with Robert Cassidy.

The executive-congressional consultation proved educational to both. Contacts with U.S. and foreign negotiators gave members a better understanding of the process and the international politics of the negotiation. U.S. negotiators obtained the benefit of hearing the views of members of Congress.

Following the conclusion of the Tokyo Round and the passage of legislation to implement its results, the House Foreign Affairs Committee reviewed the procedures by which the trade agreements were considered by Congress. The key element, the committee concluded, was the close involvement of members of Congress during the period of negotiation:

> Although the fast-track procedures tend to facilitate the legislative consideration of complex agreements by making it impossible for a minority to amend the legislation or kill it by filibuster, it is necessary also to build congressional support for the agreements during the actual negotiations. A general review ... of agreements already entered into no longer suffices.... What is required instead is greater congressional participation and consultation in determining the content of each agreement.
>
> ... The Members and selected committee staff made frequent trips to Geneva to attend negotiating sessions, to meet with officials of foreign delegations, and to consult and advise the head of the U.S. delegation. Although the administration ultimately made the hard political decisions on what U.S. concessions to make in return for foreign concessions, close congressional involvement helped insure there would be no surprises or agreements that Congress would likely oppose.[13]

Negotiating Authority: Substance

By the time the Trade Act of 1974 was being considered in the Senate, congressional sentiment concerning the need for more

---

[13]U.S. Congress, House of Representatives, Committee on Foreign Affairs, *Congress and Foreign Policy, 1979,* "Congress and Foreign Trade Policy: The Multilateral Trade Negotiations and Trade Reorganization," prepared by Raymond Ahearn, Analyst in International Trade and Finance, Economics Division, Congressional Research Service, (Washington: U.S. Government Printing Office, 1980), p. 137.

access for U.S. goods abroad was strong. The OPEC oil embargo made the country feel beleagured and out of control. Destler quotes Senator Russell Long, chairman of the Finance Committee, characterizing himself as "tired of the United States being the 'least favored nation' in a world that is full of discrimination. We can no longer expose our markets, while the rest of the world hides behind variable levies, export subsidies, import equalization fees, border taxes, cartels, government procurement practices, dumping, import quotas, and a host of other practices which effectively bar our products."[14] The OPEC oil embargo raised questions about access to supplies and thus Congress as a "principal negotiating objective" directed U.S. negotiators to seek "the negotiation of new rules and procedures designed to assure fair and equitable access to supplies."[15]

Another matter to which the Finance Committee was particularly sensitive was trade in agriculture. Agriculture had also received a good deal of attention in the report of the Williams Commission. The United States enjoys a comparative advantage in agricultural production, one which the Williams commission projected the country would not lose, rooted as it is in abundant natural resources and contemporary technology. By the mid-seventies, the trade deficits that had been predicted earlier by some trade experts had begun to show on a consistent basis; the rise in the price of imported oil, and the impact of that fact on the trade deficit figure would become more apparent as the decade continued. The country needed agricultural exports to help reduce the deficit. Barriers to U.S. agricultural exports were particularly aggravating, an aggravation compounded by the EC's aggressive use of export subsidies to dispose of its surpluses, which had the effect of displacing U.S. exports in third country markets.

U.S. agricultural constituent interests perceived Kennedy Round results on agriculture to be minimal at best. They were

---

[14]In Destler, *Making Foreign Economic Policy,* p. 169.
[15]U.S. Senate, Committee on Finance, *Trade Reform Act of 1974,* p. 81.

determined that agriculture would receive greater attention during the Tokyo Round, and believed that this result would be furthered by the linking of negotiations on agriculture and industry. To that end Congress instructed that industrial and agricultural negotiations be pursued "in conjunction with" one another.[16]

Just as U.S. agricultural export interests wanted agricultural and industrial negotiations to be related to one another, some industrial interests were concerned that gains for agriculture would come at their expense. Representatives of these interests advocated that the U.S. seek sector equivalence to be achieved by negotiating within sectors. A diluted version of a sector negotiating objective was adopted by Congress: "to the extent feasible," the negotiating authority stated, negotiators should seek equivalence in competitive opportunities by negotiating within sectors.

The opposing nature of these goals of agriculture and industry is an example of the contradictions inherent in trade policy-making and an example of the "legislative dance" between Congress and the Executive. On both issues, the Executive worked with Congress to achieve legislative language that negotiators believed would provide them with adequate flexibility.[17] Congress was able to state that the legislation directed the Executive to take into account the concerns of the U.S. private sector. And at the bargaining table, the Executive was able to point to the U.S. trade authority and suggest nonimplementation by the Congress unless certain objectives were achieved.

The Trade Act of 1974 is a detailed and precise document that directly affected not only what the United States would seek to accomplish in the Tokyo Round, but also *how* it would seek to accomplish its goals. The act reflected a "get tough" mood on the

---

[16]Reaching agreement on how to word the directive in such a way as to provide flexibility was a negotiation in itself. The words "in conjunction with" were suggested by Helene N. Wolff, wife of Alan Wolff. See Wolff, "U.S. Mandate for Trade," pp. 531–32.

[17]See especially Wolff, "U.S. Mandate for Trade," for an Executive-view analysis of the negotiating authority and the resolution of these conflicting directives.

part of the Congress, a mood growing out of the economic trials of the early seventies, but also growing out of long-term concerns and postwar policies that were increasingly irrelevant. The Williams Commission had also in many respects recommended "get tougher" stances in a U.S. approach to a round of trade negotiations. The Trade Act was also responsive to executive concerns: it was carefully crafted to allow the U.S. Executive latitude in its approach to the negotiation, and special procedures for congressional consideration of the results were devised to ameliorate U.S. trading partners' concerns about U.S. implementation. The Trade Act also addressed the concerns of the U.S. private sector, which wanted a larger and more formal role in the offering of advice on U.S. positions at the bargaining table.

4

Private Sector Support: The Advisory Committee Structure

A SIGNIFICANT ACHIEVEMENT OF THE MTN was establishment and use of an effective system for seeking advice from the private sector.[1] The system has been praised by those in the private sector who served on the various committees, by executive branch officials who set up the system and staffed it, and by members of Congress who perpetuated it by statute in the Trade Agreements Act of 1979. The process of seeking advice from industry, agriculture, and labor affected fundamental relationships between the private sector and government; a generally adversarial relationship was, for the Tokyo Round, transformed into a generally cooperative one.

Perceived need for a formal system of seeking advice from the private sector derived from the experience of the Kennedy Round. A nonstatutory system had been in effect for that trade negotiation, but advisers were dissatisfied with the quality of dialogue, or lack thereof. There was also the feeling that the

---

[1]Most of the following information on the private sector advisory process is derived from interviews with participants from government and the private sector.

private sectors of other countries had a closer relationship with their governments and that the United States needed to seek the same. At the end of the Kennedy Round, some in the private sector began suggesting to Congress that in another round of negotiations more formal advisory processes established by law would be needed.

Congress was receptive to this idea. But the establishment of the advisory system was, as one government official put it, a chicken-and-egg situation. According to several who were in the Executive at the time, Congress did not have to force the Executive to accept something that it was reluctant to accept. David Rohr, who worked on setting up the system in the Commerce Department before moving to the House Ways and Means Trade Subcommittee, has commented that executive branch officials began in 1972, 1973 and early 1974 to discuss among themselves and with some in the private sector how better to use private sector advice. A main concern was to have private sector advice factored into the government's deliberations in Washington, "rather than having some adviser sitting around (in Geneva) whose services could be called on or not depending on the whims of the negotiators." Others who served in the executive branch at the time share Rohr's assessment. Although the Nixon administration's original bill seeking negotiating authority repeated the language under which Kennedy Round advisers had served, efforts to devise a more formal system based on the recommendations of the private sector and with congressional input, particularly from staff, were underway long before the final trade legislation was passed in December 1974.

To meet concerns about the seriousness of the advisory system, procedures were devised to require communications between the government and the private sector. Additionally certain aspects of laws that would inhibit or disallow communication among committee members and between the private sector and government were waived.

The first problem, that of private sector concerns about dialogue, was met in two ways. While the government was not "of course . . . bound by the advice of any particular advisory group," the government was required to inform committees when their advice had not been taken and why. Congress also required that the president submit a report following the conclusion of the negotiation and that a section of that report be on private sector consultations and the extent to which private sector advice was or was not taken.[2]

Both the government and the private sector had concerns about confidentiality. The government was concerned that U.S. negotiating positions not be revealed to those without clearance. The private sector wanted to guard its trade secrets. In the Trade Act, Congress met these hesitations by waiving certain aspects of the Freedom of Information Act and the Federal Advisory Committee Act that provide for open meetings of government advisory committees. Certain aspects of antitrust laws had also to be waived since advisory committees brought together representatives of different companies to discuss matters that might be subject to antitrust consideration.

These waivers did not meet any strenuous opposition. One reason may be that the Trade Act was considered and passed just before the celebrated congressional reforms of the mid-seventies came into full bloom. Another reason may be that lobbying on the bill was concentrated primarily in the business community, which favored it. While the AFL–CIO opposed the Trade Act of 1974, the labor organization did so on substantive not procedural grounds. Concerns about operating in the "sunshine" simply did not resonate as they would later in the decade.

The committee structure that emerged consisted of three levels and was implemented for industry, which had the largest number of advisers and committees, for agriculture and for labor. Each level was autonomous; one did not need to gain concurrence of another. Over the course of the MTN, there were forty-five private sector advisory committees functioning, with one thousand individuals participating at one time or another.

---

[2]U.S. Senate, Committee on Finance, *The Trade Reform Act of 1974*, pp. 101–4.

The committee with the broadest perspective was the Advisory Committee for Trade Negotiations (ACTN). Members served by presidential appointment. There were forty-five on the committee, representing major producer, consumer and labor interests. Its mandate was to assess the direction and results of the Tokyo Round on the basis of the benefits to the U.S. economy as a whole.

Secondly, there were established policy advisory committees for labor, industry and agriculture. The purpose of the policy committees was to give advice and assess results on the basis of benefits to industry as a whole, agriculture and labor. Members of these committees were typically chief executive officers and other policy-oriented representatives.

Thirdly, there were the committees giving technical advice. These were the industry sector advisory committees (ISACs), the agricultural technical advisory committees (ATACs) and, originally, the labor technical advisory committees. (The labor committee structure was originally set up to operate in a manner parallel to that of industry, but with fewer committees. It evolved into one committee, guided by a steering group.) Government departments had their most consistent contact with the technical committees. These committees met more often than did the others and were more detail-oriented. There were twenty-seven ISACs corresponding to the Standard Industrial Classification system; ATACs were set up for eight commodities and in accordance with the organization of the Foreign Agricultural Service of the Department of Agriculture.

Advisers were required to undergo a security clearance; committee membership was thus strictly reserved for the member. There was no compensation for service. The government did not reimburse for travel or living expenses. Individual companies and associations paid the expenses of representatives. A number of advisers were drawn from associations with headquarters in Washington. Members of the policy and technical committees were appointed jointly by the special trade representative and the secretary of the appropriate department. Each committee chose its own chairman from among its membership, and these individuals were responsible for communicating the advice of the committee to the government. Committees met only at the call of government representatives, and government officials were required to be present at all meetings.

The private sector advisory structure was run jointly by the office of the Special Trade Representative and the international trade offices in the departments of Commerce, Agriculture and Labor. Daily administration fell to the appropriate department, and the point of official contact between the committee and the department was the "designated federal officer." STR also had a staff person assigned to the committees. These people were nicknamed "godparents." The office of the Special Trade Representative had sole responsibility for the Advisory Committee for Trade Negotiations.

Private sector advice at each level of committee was factored into the interagency decision-making process. The technical advice was not filtered through policy committees at any level. Nor was committee advice filtered through a department's internal deliberations for reaching positions to take to interagency meetings. Thus, the Department of Commerce, for instance, did not prescreen the considerations of industry committees. Nor did the department communicate to committees the position it was to take in an interagency meeting. Once an overall administration position had been taken, that position was communicated to committees, but the committees were not told individual agency positions. As one government participant put it: "We tried to avoid a situation of separating out individual agencies' positions and focused rather on the result of the interagency deliberations."

Planning, or brainstorming about what an advisory process might look like, began in the Commerce Department in early to mid-1973. Commerce held two rounds of planning meetings with private sector representatives to brief them in general about the MTN, to ask their advice on how to structure an advisory system, and to request of them nominations of individuals who might

serve. The first round, held in June 1973, was at the level of chief
executive officer. The second round of meetings was with those
at the "working level." Essentially the same issues were covered
but in more detail. The Commerce Department invited press
coverage of these meetings. Six hundred nominations for committee members emerged from this process. The Commerce
Department made additional efforts to make sure the represen-
tation of each sectoral committee was balanced, that small and
medium companies as well as large ones were represented and
that there was a geographic mix.

All of this preparatory work took place prior to the passage of
the Trade Act of 1974 so that by the time the legislation was
passed and signed into law, the advisory system was in place and
ready to go. The first set of advisory committee meetings was
held January 12, 1975.

There were several types of sessions with industry advisers.
Especially in the earlier years of the negotiation, rounds of
meetings of all ISACs were held over a period of three to five
weeks. These were held two or three times a year, and each ISAC
would meet for a full day. In the later stages of the negotiation
when there was need for a faster turnaround, the Commerce
Department established an ISAC chairmen's group which met
more frequently and at shorter notice. This group also met at
times with the IPAC; those meetings are remembered by one
ISAC chairman as an opportunity to participate in discussions
about industry as a whole, and to blend detail with policy. The
IPAC itself met formally two or three times a year.

Private sector advice on tariffs has been described as the
"heart of the advisory system." Both agricultural and industry
advisers went over the U.S. tariff schedule and other countries'
tariff schedules line by line, and they commented on the effect of
a tariff cut by the U.S. or by other countries to their sector or
commodity. Alan Wolff has described the advisers as the "source
of our negotiating. . . .

> Why should you get a tariff reduction on film from the
> Japanese? Only because your film producers would say, "We

can sell more film—give us a three-point reduction and we can sell lots more cans of film a year." No other government had [such an] elaborate process. I thought it would be a terrible thing because it got so complicated as we were drafting the '74 Trade Act. I thought it would be a millstone. It was a great strength. It did two things: It told us what we ought to do, and it made the results saleable. We had very few people opposed . . . because if we failed to achieve what they wanted, they knew why we had failed. We were being advised by a thousand private sector advisers who were in turn drawing on trade associations and their company people to say, "This is where the future lies: this is what we want." So we gave up things other people dearly wanted that we recognized were no longer of economic value.

[People compare the organization of the U.S. government for trade negotiations unfavorably with that of other countries, saying in effect,] "The U.S. government is marked by amateurism. The foreign system is composed of trained, career civil servants." Those are talented people, but they also were not as well informed as we were, with all of our amateurisms.[3]

With forty-five committees and one thousand participants, there is no yes-or-no answer to the question of whether advisers were encouraged to travel to Geneva. Some were, some were not; some government officials encouraged them, others did not. Since part of the use of advisers was political, whether or not advisers were asked to go to Geneva depended on the progress of the negotiation. At one point, for instance, members of the grains ATAC were put "on call" to travel to Geneva to reinforce U.S. negotiators.

Those advisers who did travel to Geneva were actively involved. Ambassador Alonzo McDonald, head of delegation, had devised briefing sessions and presentations for advisers. On the first day, McDonald has said, he and his staff focused on the overall goals of the MTN: "We tried to take them into our confidence not as individual practitioners . . . but as broader-

---

[3]Interview with Alan Wolff.

scale citizens." On the second day, the program focused on the advisers' specific interests and on the limits that might be negotiable: "They were on the scene; they had access to us. I would assemble for them the chief negotiators and introduce them. After they made their points, we said 'Let's begin to talk about what we might be able to get.'"[4] One adviser who had also served as adviser during the Kennedy Round, and who had been dissatisfied with that experience, commented that he felt his time had been well used when he travelled to the negotiation.

Participants in the advisory process, from the government and from the private sector, express satisfaction with their experiences. Government officials take pride that a program as large as the advisory system with potential for interagency turf battles and disputes, and with potential for showmanship at the expense of substance, worked well. Advisers found the process cumbersome, requiring a great amount of time and commitment, and yet they were satisfied with the quality of the dialogue with the government and with the governmental consideration given their recommendations. During the period of congressional consideration of the results of the MTN, government officials pointed to the reports of the advisory committees as evidence that what was negotiated was supported by the private sector. It is true that there were very few committees that issued a negative opinion on the entire negotiation. Yet a closer reading of the reports reveals lukewarm support for the agreements with a heavy dose of "let's wait and see." Private sector enthusiasm resulted from their experience as members of advisory committees. This is an accolade to those civil servants who staffed the program and to the governmental leadership that encouraged its establishment.

Two concerns of some who were close to the MTN proved unfounded. There were predictions of massive leaks of classified information. Only two occurred, both from private advisers who were chastised by their peers. Another concern was that close

---

[4]Interview with Alonzo McDonald.

involvement of the private sector would lead to the private sector's dictating to the government what positions to take. Those who held this view predicted that, in particular, the congressionally-mandated requirement that the the government report to advisers whether their advice had been taken, and if not why not, would facilitate such a "tyranny" of the private sector. Most who have reflected on the MTN process conclude that the fear was unfounded and the accountability mechanism not pernicious. They point out that while committee advice was factored into the government's decision-making process, positions taken were those of the government. That the government as a whole reached a particular position was reinforced through the practice of reporting to committees what emerged from the interagency process, and *not* what individual departments concluded.

The various departments and the office of the Special Trade Representative seem to have managed their "joint custody" well. Both the appropriate department and the STR's office sent representatives to all committee meetings. Committee members were very aware that government officials in STR were available to them as readily as were those in the "constituency" department. Advisers were appointed jointly by the special trade representative and the secretary of commerce, agriculture or labor. Committee chairmen received communications from STR Strauss or Deputy STR Wolff advising them of positions taken in the interagency process, which the office of the STR chaired at each of its three levels.

There are several factors that various participants both from government and from the private sector have identified as contributing to the success of the MTN advisory process. One is the waiver of the "sunshine" laws. Without that waiver, most say, the committees could not and would not have operated. Sunshine laws, according to this argument, work to box people into positions. A position that has been stated for the public record is difficult to amend. Another factor contributing to success was the fact that members served with no recompense or even reimbursement of expenses. Those on committees were there because of a commitment. Finally, committee member selection was accomplished without respect to political affiliation; there was no party loyalty test. This feature of the advisory system was changed in the Reagan administration and, many say, the system has suffered because of it.

A benefit of the system that also was a factor contributing to its success was the education of the participants. Advisers were at times presented with the situation of the government and asked for advice on how to resolve it from a broad perspective, not just from that of their sector. This had the effect of creating empathy for the enormity of the government's task and blurring the "adversarial" relationship between the private sector and the government. With the exception of a few industrial and agricultural sectors, this set of relationships was carried into the bill-writing phase of the MTN process.

The experience of the labor advisory committee was somewhat different from that of industry and agriculture committees. In general, labor tended not to "negotiate" with the government. The preferred position of the grains ATAC, for instance, was opposition to a commodity agreement for coarse grains; however, it also worked out what it could live with were a commodity agreement to be accepted by the United States. The labor committee tended not to work out fallback positions. Furthermore, agreements of benefit to labor interests were being devised outside the context of the negotiaton *per se* under what some have termed Strauss's "divide and conquer" strategy, meaning that Strauss in effect "bought off" some labor interests by trading special concessions or government aid for support or nonresistance to the trade package.

5

Obstacles: Agriculture and Textiles

T HROUGHOUT THE NEGOTIATING PERIOD, Congress and the private sector were looking over the shoulders of the American negotiators. In fact, negotiations with these two domestic elements were as important to the success of the agreements as were the negotiations in Geneva. Probably no other participants were required to be as constantly attentive to the domestic scene as were those in the United States delegation.

The first three-to-four years of the Tokyo Round moved slowly. The U.S. Executive had expected to have authority to negotiate by early in 1974; that authority was not in fact provided until January 1975, though organizational activities did go forward.

For the formal negotiations in Geneva, a Trade Negotiations Committee was established composed of all countries participating in the round, GATT and non-GATT members alike. With a membership of some one hundred nations and three hundred delegates, its purpose was not to serve as a setting for the negotiations themselves, but rather to elaborate and put into effect detailed negotiating plans; to establish appropriate negotiating procedures; and to supervise the progress of the negotiations.[1]

The TNC set up groups and subgroups within which to carry out the substance of the negotiation. From the start, the agricultural negotiation posed difficulties. An agricultural group was established, but reaching agreement on what it would cover and what issues pertaining to agriculture would be negotiated in other groups, proved to be a stumbling block. How, for instance, would agricultural tariffs be handled? Would a single formula for industrial and agricultural tariffs be devised? Would agricultural tariffs be negotiated in the agricultural group or in the tariffs group?

"[T]hroughout 1976, agriculture in the MTN continued to be an area marked by contrasting U.S./EC views. The United States, as required by Section 103 of the Trade Act of 1974, is committed to negotiating agriculture in conjunction with industry. The EC, on the other hand, insists that the two areas be negotiated separately, contending that its Common Agricultural Policy [CAP] is a domestic matter not subject to negotiation." A procedural compromise had been negotiated at the end of 1975 providing for "notifications and consultations involving agricultural products not covered by specific subgroups [i.e., meat, dairy, grains],"[2] but after that accomplishment the issue remained in stalemate until 1977.

Progress in general in the MTN was slow in 1976 as "major countries . . . [were taking] a cautious attitude . . . because of slow economic recovery"[3] and prospective elections in the United States and in other principal participating countries including Japan, West Germany and the United Kingdom. Although fast-moving negotiating did not begin until 1978, with an important procedural breakthrough in 1977, work did go forward in Ge-

---

[1]Information on the framework is found in GATT, *Tokyo Round*, Report of the Director-General, pp. 8–9, and in U.S. Senate, Committee on Finance, *Trade Agreements Act of 1979*, pp. 2–3.

[2]*International Economic Report of the President*, 1977, p. 45.

[3]Ibid., p. 44.

neva. It was during this period that drafts of codes of conduct on nontariff barriers were produced and circulated. Alan Wolff has described the process of negotiating on NTBs in these terms:

> We finally learned that the way you negotiate is, you say, "Now, we have this problem. Do you think that's a problem?" They'd say yes or no and you'd work very gradually towards consensus on the problem, consensus on approaches to solving the problem, and then approaches on the solution itself.[4]

Jimmy Carter was elected president in 1976. He nominated Robert S. Strauss for the position of special trade representative. Strauss' nomination was unanimously approved by the Senate and he took office in March 1977.

Robert Strauss, former chairman of the Democratic National Committee, is a well-known politician from Texas. He is widely credited with reuniting the Democratic Party after the divisions of 1972, and thus making possible its victory in 1976. He became a loyal supporter of Jimmy Carter, who had few close associates among Washington insiders. As such, Strauss stood in direct contrast to the "Georgia Mafia" that made up Carter's inner circle. The Carter team had campaigned on an anti-Washington, antipolitician theme. Once inside the White House, they had difficulty reconciling that image with the political requirements of working the system to get things done.

Strauss helped bridge that gap. He knew how to accomplish the goals he set, and he knew whose help he would need to do it. He brought to the Carter White House an extensive network of well-established relationships with members of Congress.

Unlike some of the members of the Carter adminstration who seemed almost embarrassed to be involved in the political process, Strauss reveled in it. And he had learned long before serving as STR the most important lesson successful and contented politicians must know: you never get everything you want.

---

[4]Interview with Alan Wolff.

Writing about the trade agreements during the phase of congressional consideration, he in effect summarized his philosophy:

> We must beware of well-meaning purists. Their measure of
> progress is not the giant step forward we take from where we
> stand, but the gap still remaining to achieve the ideal.
> Although I admire their intelligence and dedication, I do not
> have much patience with their position. Their tactical thrust
> is often to attack the "politics of the deal" and the process of
> developing a political consensus that can assure national
> support and congressional approval. They imply that politics
> is something dirty and improper rather than recognizing that
> progress in a democracy is built on accommodating different
> views from all sections of our society. You will hear more and
> more of "Bob Strauss, the pragmatist and politician."[5]

Strauss's instinct was to set about "developing a political consensus" internationally to relaunch the stalled negotiation and domestically to achieve its acceptance. He did this, he and others say, by a mixture of bullying, cajoling, reassuring, pacifying and preaching. There was not a week, he says, that he was not in a "major communication center" talking about trade to one group or another. Strauss describes the process as one of building personal relationships and trust; his counterparts "became people whose burdens and troubles I shared, and they shared mine."[6] Former Deputy STR Wolff describes Strauss' "great strength" as "understanding what the other fellow had to have on the other side of the table. . . .

> You can't bully people into doing what's contrary to what
> they know they can deliver. And his great talent was to find
> that point of maximum progress which was consistent with
> another country's interest. If they went beyond that . . . you
> would be getting an agreement on something they couldn't

---

[5]Robert S. Strauss, "The Achievements of the Tokyo Round," *Washington Post,* 20 March 1979, A17.

[6]Interview with Robert Strauss.

possibly deliver, so you wouldn't have an agreement. He found what he would describe in "Texan" as their choking point.[7]

Strauss was also comfortable with members of Congress. He had a great many friends on Capitol Hill who had faith that Robert Strauss would not sell out U.S. economic interests. Strauss's political savvy and ability allowed him to use the "Congress card" to push trading partners to their "choking point" after which he would testify to Congress that progress had been made and restrictive actions would not, after all, be necessary.

Until July of 1977 organization matters went forward within the U.S. government. In July, Ambassador Wolff "went on the road" to a series of bilateral discussions—with the "ice bloc" countries of Sweden, Norway, Denmark and Finland, and with Switzerland, Canada, Japan, and the European Community—to talk about what might be achieved in the MTN. As part of that effort Strauss went to Brussels for his first meeting with the European Commission:

> He came into the meeting and looked over the agenda and he said, "Well, where's the press conference?" And they said there wasn't one; what would one announce? And Strauss said, "Well, I'll either praise or denounce the results of what we do here today." [A press conference was scheduled] and an initial draft of what might be announced was tabled by one of the European negotiators. Strauss threw it back across the table and said, "This could have been written two years ago; this is of no value." He eked progress out of that meeting. And we were moving.[8]

What evolved from that meeting was a framework for the continuation and completion of the MTN. The framework was a

---

[7]Interview with Alan Wolff.
[8]Ibid.

four-phase plan with deadlines for the completion of each phase.

In the first phase, countries would agree upon a general tariff plan including: (a) a tariff-cutting formula; (b) specific directives for treatment of agriculture; (c) a method of dealing with countries not subscribing to the tariff-cut formula; (d) a specific statement on treatment of less-developed countries. The second phase would consist of the tabling of requests for: (a) tariff cuts on agricultural goods; (b) nontariff measures not the subject of codes of conduct; (c) tariff cuts by countries not subscribing to the tariff-cutting formula. In the third phase draft texts of codes of conduct for nontariff barriers would be tabled, and in the final phase countries would table their offers in response to the previously tabled requests.

The goal was to complete these four phases by January of 1978. Requests were to be submitted in November 1977 and offers in January 1978. Though deadlines slipped, this plan set in July 1977 was followed for the remainder of the negotiation.

The basis for the breakthrough was an agreement on how to proceed on agricultural negotiations. The European Community would not agree to negotiate in such a manner as to undermine the cornerstone of the Common Agricultural Policy, the variable levy. Negotiating agricultural and industrial tariffs together would interfere with the variable levy. Strauss assured EC delegates that the U.S. would not seek to attack the CAP. The U.S. and EC agreed on language stating that agriculture and industry issues would be negotiated "in parallel." Strauss explained this to mean that while they would not be negotiated "in the same room," the United States would assess the results as one package. Resolution of the issue at the political level opened the way for the request-offer arrangement on agricultural items to be agreed to and the Tokyo Round moved forward.

The work of the MTN was substantially completed in 1978. In November 1977, negotiators had reached agreement on a tariff-cutting formula, and countries had tabled their requests. In mid-January, countries tabled their offers; January 28 marked the ceremonial opening of active bargaining. The principal countries of the negotiation—major industrialized countries—were working toward having in hand a substantive document for heads of state to consider at the upcoming Bonn economic summit which was to be held July 16–17. That goal was achieved when on July 13 a Framework of Understanding was issued by the European Economic Community, the United States, Japan, Switzerland, New Zealand, Canada, the Nordic countries and Austria. The developing countries issued their own statement disavowing the Framework of Understanding and asserting that an adequate understanding of the status of the negotiation could be had only with the participation of all countries involved in it.[9]

---

[9]The importance of developing countries to the world economy and the world's commerce had been stressed throughout the period prior to the opening of the Tokyo Round in, for instance, the reports of the Rey group and the Williams Commission. Participation in the Tokyo Round was open to non-GATT members, many of whom were LDCs. The Tokyo Declaration had emphasized the need for more LDC participation in institutional arrangements governing trade, while at the same time acknowledging development goals and the importance of LDCs' not assuming obligations that would undermine those goals.

One goal of the developing countries was the inclusion within the GATT framework of the legitimacy of the the concept of "special and differential" treatment for LDCs. Acknowledgment of special and differential treatment within GATT would allow LDCs legally to take actions that otherwise would be illegal. The United States held the position that the concept of graduation was a necessary corollary to special and differential treatment. Graduation recognizes that development status changes and provides for the removal of LDCs from the category receiving special benefits. LDCs opposed inclusion of graduation, but they lost their case.

There was also a division between developed and developing countries over the matter of a safeguards code. This code negotiation was not concluded because agreement could not be reached. As the decade of the seventies wore on, industrialized countries became more concerned about the disruptive effect of imports from LDCs. The European Community was interested in negotiating a code that would allow "selective" safeguard action against imports from particular countries. While such a code would be in direct opposition to the MFN principle, *de facto* selectivity had been operating for years. An argument in favor of selectivity in a code was that if the rules were changed, governments would not then be operating contrary to GATT. An argument in opposition was that legally sanctioning the use of practices such as selectivity would lead to breakdown of GATT principles and ideals. Although a safeguards code allowing selectivity was not completed, the negotiation of bilateral "voluntary" export restraints is common.

In addition to substantive complaints, LDCs objected to procedures. Although such journals as *The Economist* reported on extensive efforts to brief LDC representatives and keep them informed of developments, LDCs were not consulted or negotiated with. This

Beginning in late summer and continuing through the balance of 1978, actions of the U.S. Congress interfered with the progress of the MTN and its conclusion. The congressional activity involved the interests of the textile and apparel industries.

The industrial sector of textiles and apparel in the United States is a major employer which in 1979 provided work to some 2.2 million people.[10] A labor-intensive industry, it employs many low-skilled workers and has a reputation for employing newly-entered immigrants to the country. It is also one of the first industries that countries that have begun to industrialize traditionally establish. At the beginning of the postwar Japanese recovery, textiles were the first wave of "disruptive" exports entering the U.S. market. Clothing imports from the Philippines, Taiwan, China and India are now common in the United States.

Textiles have been afforded special protection from imports. In 1961 the United States and other industrialized countries negotiated with developing country exporters the Short-Term Agreement on Cotton Textiles. The Short-Term Agreement was replaced with the Long-Term Agreement, which in turn was replaced in 1974 with the Multi-Fiber Agreement covering synthetics. The MFA allows governments to restrict imports in ways that otherwise would be contrary to the GATT. The MFA is an "umbrella" arrangement for bilateral quotas on exports/ imports. It also establishes a rate of "orderly" growth in textile and apparel trade, that is, it manages trade in textiles and apparel.

Special arrangements for the textile industry have been made

---

was particularly true with respect to the essentially U.S./EC negotiation leading to the resolution of the problem of the treatment of agriculture, and making possible the subsequent progress in the negotiation as a whole. While the MTN was on paper the largest negotiation that had ever occurred, it was in reality a negotiation among the "Big Three"—the U.S., the EC and Japan.

[10]In 1979 production worker employment in mills stood at 771,000. Employment of production workers in apparel factories was 1,117,000. Nonproduction worker employment in textiles and apparel was 312,000. U.S. Bureau of the Census, *Statistical Abstract of the United States: 1981* (102d edition), Washington, D.C., 1981.

for political reasons during the course of overall trade negotiations; indeed, some observers comment that industry representatives see trade negotiations as an opportunity to negotiate
more protection from the U.S. government. Prior to the Tokyo
Round, certain categories of especially import-sensitive textiles
were excluded from the negotiation by the U.S., but since the
United States had the highest textile tariffs in the world, it was
not possible to have a tariff negotiation without having U.S.
textiles on the table, and in fact the U.S. had made an offer to
reduce by some 25.5 percent.[11]

The year 1978, in which intensive bargaining in Geneva took
place, was an election year for the United States. Strauss's overall
MTN "sales" strategy had already taken that fact into account;
the negotiation was deliberately timed to end *after* the November
election so that members would not have to vote on a trade
liberalization package before the election. The fact that 1978 was
an election year influenced congressional action on two measures that were technically separate but politically related and
important to the textile industry.

The first issue was a measure to exclude textiles from tariff
reduction negotiations. Its sponsor was Senator Ernest Hollings
from South Carolina, a state in which there is a great deal of
textile production. The second issue related to the authority
granted by Congress in the Trade Act of 1974 to the Secretary of
the Treasury to waive the imposition of countervailing duties on
subsidized imports. The waiver authority was running out as of
January 3, 1979, and the Europeans insisted on an extension
before continuing the negotiation.

The Hollings amendment to remove U.S. textile tariffs from
the bargaining table was in one way not serious. It was not
serious in the sense that no one expected that textile tariffs would
in fact be removed. It was however serious in two other ways: it
allowed Senator Hollings the opportunity to take the lead in
support of the interests of an industry important to his state, and

---

[11]"American Protectionism," *The Economist,* 7 October 1978, pp. 97–98.

it was part of the political pressure on the administration to "come up with something" for the textile industry.

Hollings' amendment was offered in October 1978 to a bill reauthorizing the Export-Import Bank. Despite Strauss's warning—"If we don't keep textiles on the table, others will take from the table items essential to us, and the talks could well collapse [and] in particular what is jeopardized is our agricultural expansion"[12]—the amendment was accepted. The EXIM bill was ultimately crushed under the weight of additional nongermane amendments.

Senator Hollings then offered his amendment to a throwaway bill authorizing the General Services Administration to dispose of $24 million worth of Carson City silver dollars. The bill passed the Senate; the amendment was accepted by the House in conference and the conference report was accepted by both the full House and Senate. President Carter vetoed the bill after the November election, which everyone knew he would do, and the Hollings Amendment, but not the textile issue, was dead.

During this same period the legislation to extend the countervailing duty waiver came before the Congress. Extending the authority to waive countervailing duties was a sensitive issue for Congress to have to consider in an election year because the extension was in effect a decision not to enforce a U.S. unfair trade law. Especially in an election year, members prefer criticizing the Executive for laxness in defending U.S. industry against unfair trade to participating actively in the suspension of U.S. unfair trade laws.

Robert Strauss was aware of this particular difficulty. In September of 1978 he had begun discussions with congressional leaders about how to handle the waiver authority. At that time, House Speaker Thomas P. O'Neill and others counseled against seeking an extension before adjournment.[13] Because the waiver

---

[12]As quoted in "Carter Officials Say Congress's Actions Could Impede U.S. Aides at Trade Talks," by Richard J. Levine, *Wall Street Journal,* 6 October 1978, p. 4.

[13]"Carter May Seek to Extend Right to Waive Countervailing Duties on Certain Imports," *Wall Street Journal,* 22 September 1978, p. 31.

would expire before Congress reconvened in mid-January 1979 and because the Europeans were pressuring Strauss for the extension, the decision was made to seek a waiver extension bill. Strauss testified in favor of the waiver on October 5, 1978.

The fact that 1978 was an election year for members of the House and some senators meant that Congress would adjourn early in order for members to campaign. The press of business that often accompanies an early adjournment is an opportunity for legislative maneuvering, and in the Senate for the decoration of "Christmas tree" bills. A Christmas tree is a bill that has attached to its core measure a number of nongermane amendments. Christmas trees may originate only in the Senate since the House has rules disallowing nongermane amendments. Senator Russell Long, the chairman of the Finance Committee, was famous for his ability to have passed in the last hours before adjournment bills that may not have passed under other circumstances. Long's mastery of timing was legendary, and as *Congressional Quarterly* put it that year, "The Last Train's Leaving the Station and Long's in Charge—As Usual."

Thus when Strauss decided to seek an extension of the countervailing duty waiver in early October, he was doing so close to adjournment, a fact that he no doubt hoped would work in his favor. The waiver extension was in its short but complicated life attached to two bills: one to increase price supports for sugar producers and one to strengthen adjustment assistance. It was not coincidental that the Carter administration was on record as opposing both bills.

The sugar price support bill was already enmeshed in another legislative drama. Because of the Carter administration's opposition to higher support prices, Senator Frank Church was withholding his subcommittee's consideration of the International Sugar Agreement that the administration favored. Church, from Idaho, favored the higher support level because of production of sugar beets in the state.

The sentiment in the House was also for an increase in sugar support prices, and on October 6 (one day after Strauss had testified for the waiver extension), the House passed a price support bill. In the Senate, the Finance Committee added the CVD waiver extension to its version of the bill. The committee had worked with the administration to come up with provisions the administration would accept, and as further "veto proofing" it had attached the waiver extension measure.

This compromise bill, however, was rejected by the House in conference committee. The basis for opposition was in part dissatisfaction with the price support compromise. Some members opposed the bill because the waiver extension was attached to it. Textile interests were opposed to the waiver in the absence of meaningful actions on the part of the Executive to aid the industry. The Hollings amendment could be vetoed. It was wise strategically for the industry to work toward keeping from the administration something it wanted.

There was in the final days of the 95th Congress another attempt on the part of Congress to pass the waiver extension. This time it was attached to the adjustment assistance bill. The House had passed the adjustment assistance bill on September 8. The Senate took it up on the last day of the Congress, October 15. On the floor, senators transformed the bill into a Christmas tree, with many nongermane amendments, and with a partially germane amendment, the CVD waiver extension. The Senate then sent the bill back to the House where the Ways and Means Committee stripped it of most of the Senate amendments, but not the waiver extension, added some of its own and reported it to the floor. The bill was passed easily by the full House, but time was short; in fact it was the second to the last bill acted upon before the House adjourned. The Finance Committee did not support the amendments attached by the House, but there was no time for further back and forth. The situation was for the Senate to take it or leave it. Senate Majority Leader Robert Byrd made the decision that it should be left, despite a phone call from President Carter asking that the Senate take it up because of the waiver extension provision.[14]

---

[14]The account of the countervailing-duty-waiver extension is derived from the reports in *Congressional Quarterly* throughout the period. In particular, see "Looking for a Ship

Between January 3, 1979 when the original waiver authority expired, and March 1979 when Congress passed waiver extension authority, an administrative arrangement was developed to handle the pending countervailing duties and the MTN went forward. Also during that period Strauss and the textile industry came to an agreement on a package of government actions to help the industry. Announced February 15, the provisions consisted of an administration pledge to control disruptive import surges; to negotiate bilateral agreements with new suppliers such as China; and to monitor textile imports continuously on a global basis. Some in the State Department opposed the package, especially the provisions relating to China. The United States had at the end of 1978 normalized relations with China. They feared, correctly, that protective actions on the part of the U.S. against Chinese exports would damage relations.

On March 1, 1979 the House of Representatives approved the waiver extension on a voice vote. On April 12, 1979 negotiators initialed the results of the Tokyo Round.

* * * * *

When U.S. negotiators left Geneva, they took with them the results of the Tokyo Round: an average tariff cut of some 33 percent; six codes of conduct on various nontariff measures; an agreement on civil aircraft; negotiated changes in the GATT framework, and consultative agreements on meat and dairy products. On agriculture, negotiators had not been able to dislodge the CAP, but they had concluded a subsidies code, which included provisions that it was hoped would bring discipline to the use of export subsidies. The standards code was also of use to agriculture. The code required signatories to "make known in advance any proposed changes in regulations that set

---

Leaving Port in the Final Hours," *Congressional Quarterly,* 21 October 1978, p. 3023. For the influence of the textile industry on the sugar legislation, see "Sugar Legislation Dies," *Congressional Quarterly,* 21 October 1978, p. 3087. For a report on Senator Long's skill with "adjournment bills," see "The Last Train's Leaving the Station and Long's in Charge—As Usual," *Congressional Quarterly,* 7 October 1978, pp. 2737–39.

product standards and specifications, including packaging, marking, and labeling regulations, so that interested traders will have an opportunity to comment on the proposed changes before they are finally adopted."[15] Tariff and quota concessions for U.S. agricultural exports covered $3.8 billion of exports in 1976 value.[16] Outside the formal Geneva negotiations, but within the context of the MTN, Strauss had concluded with the Japanese agreements for increased Japanese quotas on some agricultural goods, mainly beef and citrus.

Among the concessions offered by the United States were the addition of an injury test to the U.S. countervailing duty law. One of the reasons U.S. trading partners found the U.S. law so aggravating was that countervailing duties were authorized regardless of whether the imports caused injury to domestic industry; furthermore, the U.S. law was a violation of the GATT. How the new injury test would be framed became an important issue during congressional consideration of the implementing legislation. The United States also expanded its quotas on imported cheeses, and conceded the "wine gallon" method of customs valuation for liquor. The "wine gallon" method of taxation made it economically disadvantageous for foreign exporters to export already-bottled liquor. U.S. distillers were thus advantaged by a nontariff barrier.

Tariff agreements became effective with no implementing action on the part of Congress. The other measures required congressional approval.

---

[15]U.S. Department of Agriculture, Foreign Agricultural Service, *Report on Agricultural Concessions in the Multilateral Trade Negotiations,* June 1981, p. 1.

[16]Ibid.

6

The Results of the MTN:
The Trade Agreements Act
of 1979

D ESPITE THE CLOSE CONSULTATION that had been maintained with Congress through the negotiating period, a lengthy and, at times, uncertain procedure awaited the results of the international negotiation. At one point, it was necessary to renegotiate internationally one part of the agreements, that relating to the government procurement code. Nevertheless, despite problems, the results of the Tokyo Round were implemented via legislation passed by both houses of Congress and signed into law by President Carter.

There were several unique features to the legislative process of the Trade Agreements Act of 1979. Some of these features had been crafted as part of the Trade Act of 1974. Others resulted from negotiations between the jurisdictional committees, especially the Senate Finance Committee, and the Office of the Special Trade Representative.

The features provided by the 1974 legislation were presidential notification ninety days prior to entering trade agreements of U.S. intent to do so; executive branch submission to Congress of proposed legislation to implement the trade agreements; restrictions on the amount of time committees could consider the legislation, with an automatic discharge provision should committees fail to report; and a rule disallowing amendments from the floor. Once the implementing legislation was on the floor of the House or Senate, the vote was up or down.

These provisions had a number of implications, both for Congress—in effect, the House Ways and Means and Senate Finance committees—and for the Office of the Special Trade Representative. The Executive used the ninety-day notification period to determine if there were portions of agreements that needed to be renegotiated, and to discuss what might be in an implementing bill. After the agreements were initialed on April 12, attention was focused on writing the legislation. Because the legislation was nonamendable, and the trade agreements not subject to renegotiation, agreement between Congress and the Executive and between the two committees had to be reached *before* the legislation was officially submitted to Congress. The process of committee consideration of legislative content was dubbed a "nonmarkup," a markup being a jurisdictional committee's change of proposed legislation. Differences between the Ways and Means and Finance committee bills were resolved in a "nonconference."

The legislative process through which the Trade Agreements Act of 1979 travelled included all the major elements of a more usual bill-writing endeavor. Parts of the process, especially closed "markup" and "conference" sessions, were reminiscent of congressional procedure before "sunshine" reforms were introduced in the mid-seventies. The timing was, however, very different. As can be seen from the chart on the next following page detailing the legislative timetable, formal legislation was not submitted to Congress until June 19, 1979, by which time all decisions had been made.

Robert Cassidy, who was at the time of the Tokyo Round counsel to the Senate Finance Committee, has described the MTN bill-writing process in an essay, "Negotiating about Negotations."[1] The genesis for much of the procedure developed between the committees and STR was interest on the part of members of the commmittees in retaining effective control over the bill-writing process. The Trade Act of 1974 had specified that the president would submit a bill to Congress and that the bill would be nonamendable. It could not specify how an acceptable, nonamendable bill might be written.

In April 1978 the Finance Committee staff had begun to address the problem of how the committees could work their will before the nonamendable bill was introduced. The committee staff suggestion was that the bill be drafted on the Hill. STR acceded to the suggestion and the agreement was confirmed in an exchange of letters between Senator Ribicoff, chairman of the Finance Committee Subcommittee on International Trade, and Ambassador Strauss.

Shortly after the president transmitted the notification of intent to enter, the administration sent the international agreements to Congress. The staffs of the Ways and Means and Finance committees developed "spread sheets" detailing current law, administration proposals and the relevant portions of the trade agreements, and proposals of members of Congress, if any. The trade agreements and implementing proposals concerned matters that fell within the jurisdictions of a number of committees. Under normal circumstances, the agreements and implementing proposals would have been referred to those committees for consideration as well as to the committees with primary jurisdiction. Ways and Means sought and received permission to waive joint referral, and instead invited members of the appropriate committees to participate in discussions as pertinent. In the Senate the agriculture and commerce com-

---

[1]Robert C. Cassidy, "Negotiating about Negotiations: The Geneva Multilateral Trade Talks," in *The Tethered Presidency: Congressional Restraints on Executive Power,* Thomas M. Franck, ed. (New York: New York University Press, 1981), pp. 264–82.

Legislative Timetable: Trade Agreements Act of 1979

Administration	House Ways & Means	Senate Finance	House & Senate
Jan. 4, 1979: Notice of intent to enter trade agreements	February: Organization of Ways & Means for 96th Congress; adopt structure for considering legislation	Feb. 21–22: Finance Committee hearings on implementation of MTN	
	March 12: Begin executive session with STR & other administration officials; continue meetings on March 13–14, 19–21; April 3–5 and 10; May 1–3, 8 and 16; 47.5 hours	March 6–8, 15–26: Executive session with STR & other administration officials; sessions cont'd April 4–5; May 2–3	
April 12: U.S. enters into trade agreements; text of agreements made public	April 23–27: Public hearings, 18.5 hours of testimony	May 8: Press release detailing Senate recommendations	April 23: Text of agreements published jointly by Ways & Means and Senate Finance
	May 18: Ways & Means publishes recommendations on implementing legislation		May 21–23: Trade Subcommittee & Finance Committee meet to resolve differences in implementing legislation ("nonconference")
			May 24: Vanik and Long issue joint press release detailing resolution of House & Senate differences and announcing completion of consultations with administration
June 19: President Carter transmits implementing package to Congress	June 21: Ways & Means reports unanimously from committee	July 10–11: Subcttee. on International Trade hearings	
	July 11: HR 4537 approved by House 395–7	July 23: Senate passes HR 4537 on vote of 90–4	
July 26: Carter signs into law PL96-39			

mittees met to consider those issues and legislative proposals within their jurisdictions.

Executive sessions held in March, April and May provided the forum for members and STR and other administration officials to discuss the measures "necessary or appropriate" to implement the trade agreements. Decisions reached in those closed-door meetings provided the substance of the bills. In his essay, Cassidy has described those meetings:

> ... [C]ommittee staff first presented the material. Then administration officials and members of the committee discussed the proposal until agreement was reached. Whenever disagreements arose, the committees directed their staffs to sit down with the administration and "work something out." [If votes had to be taken], more often than not, the administration lost those votes and some other proposal prevailed. . . .
>
> Although many administration officials initially viewed the committee sessions as hand-holding exercises, the results of which could be ignored, they eventually came to take the process very seriously and fought vigorously to sustain their position.[2]

Although STR staff had been reluctant to agree to congressional drafting of the bill, their acquiescence ultimately proved beneficial to the office. As Harry Lamar, who was the Ways and Means Committee's top staff person for trade, has pointed out, the fact that the draft came from the Hill insulated STR from intense and potentially divisive interagency disputes.[3] Officials from other departments participated in the executive sessions, and the focus became negotiating for points with the committees rather than negotiating with STR. STR could deflect other agencies' criticisms by invoking the "mood of Congress," just as Congress had deflected criticism or deferred trade-restrictive action while "STR negotiates" or "Bob works it out."

---

[2]Ibid., p. 275.
[3]Interview with Harry Lamar.

An element of the legislative process that was not easily accommodated in this special process was the holding of public hearings. Hearings were not in fact scheduled until the committees came under "considerable pressure," as Cassidy puts it, to hold them. It was possible for witnesses to comment on the trade agreements themselves because detailed descriptions had been published in the *Federal Register* on January 4. Some of the witnesses were members of the private sector advisory groups; in addition to substance, they were able to comment on the advisory system process. However, because discussions to implement the actual agreements were held in executive session, public witnesses did not know what specific actions were under consideration. Thus, for instance, witnesses knew that the United States had accepted an injury test for its countervailing duty law. But for the bill-writing process, the key question was the *definition* of injury, not the fact of an injury test. How to define injury was being discussed in closed committee rooms. This led to some complaints about being left out of the process.[4]

The drafting group established to write the trade legislation produced a comprehensive bill which STR submitted informally to Congress on June 5, 1979. Whether to write a bill encompassing all the agreements or to write several bills was a question addressed earlier. A comprehensive bill was chosen because it was thought that "stronger" agreements would support "weaker" ones, and that it would be harder to vote "no" since a vote against a comprehensive bill would be a vote against the entire MTN effort in which Congress had been so intimately involved. Formal legislation was sent to the Hill on June 19, and House and Senate action quickly followed.

On July 11, HR 4537 was adopted by the House of Representatives on a vote of 395–7. On July 23, the Senate approved the measure, 90–4. President Carter signed the bill into law on July

---

[4]See Clyde Farnsworth, "Pressure Mounting on Trade Packagers: Lobbyists Pursue Special Waivers; Deadline Nears," *New York Times,* 25 March 1979, Section III, p. 1.

26, and the Trade Agreements Act of 1979 became Public Law 96–39.

*   *   *   *   *

"There is not much fascination," said Barber Conable, ranking Republican on the Ways and Means Committee, "in a finally achieved consensus. . . . There is very little drama in this moment which has been a long time coming to the floor of the House."[5] The *Washington Post* barely noted final passage of the trade legislation, which was passed by the widest margin in U.S. history. The trade bill's low profile was not coincidental. Robert Strauss's strategy was to develop enough support, no matter the degree of enthusiasm, to pass the bill with little controversy. Those few issues that did have potential for controversy were defused as quickly as possible. They were the matter of small and minority business set-asides; the subsidies/countervailing duty code; enlarged cheese quotas and the "wine gallon" matter. The latter two achieved little public attention.

The first issue related to the government procurement code, negotiated to chip away at the practice of preferential bidding for domestic producers on government contracts. In the United States, the federal preference was embodied largely in the Buy American Act, but other programs would be affected too. To implement the code agreement, those laws had to be amended. As negotiated, the code provisions would apply to federal government contracts of $190,000 or more.

In March, it became clear that implementation of the government procurement code would affect programs designed to benefit small and minority-owned businesses. These programs, known as set-asides, reserve for small and for minority-owned businesses a certain portion of government procurement con-

---

[5]As quoted in "House Passes Big Trade Bill; Overwhelming Vote Reflects 'Finally Achieved Consensus,'" *Congressional Quarterly* 37 (14 July 1982):1406.

tracts. Representatives of those businesses, their trade associations, and congressional supporters, particularly members of the House Small Business Subcommittee and a study group on minority enterprises, quickly rallied to apply pressure on the administration to protect the set-asides. Strauss's original response was that the programs would not be affected since the code applied to contracts of $190,000 or more,[6] and that, moreover, additional export opportunities would become available because of the code. "He withdrew that defense when it was established that the average minority set-aside is $222,357 and the average set-aside for manufacturers is $526,821."[7] Proponents of the set-aside pointed out further that export opportunities were of little value to businesses that have difficulty competing in the domestic market; to help them compete and become established was seen as a socially useful goal and the reason for the programs in the first place. Strauss agreed to renegotiate the code.

The government procurement code was the only international agreement that had to be renegotiated. Participants in and analysts of the negotiation point to that fact as a demonstration that the private sector and congressional consultation systems worked. It also demonstrated the ability of the administration to be adaptable to congressional concerns. "I'm delighted with the development," Parren Mitchell, chairman of a House study group on minority enterprises said. "It shows a responsiveness by Mr. Strauss and will facilitate passage of the trade bill."[8]

A second issue was the countervailing duty question. Throughout the MTN, negotiators were very aware of the po-

---

[6]Trade policy officials in earlier administrations catalogued small business set-asides as part of U.S. law that constituted an NTB; see Marks and Malmgren, "Negotiating Nontariff Distortions to Trade."

[7]U.S. Congress, Senate, Committee on Finance, Subcommittee on International Trade, *Hearing on S 1376,* Statement of the National Tool, Die and Precision Machinery Association and Small Business Legislative Council (part 2 of 21, 96th Congress, 1*st* session, 11 July 1979, p. 549.

[8]As quoted in "Small Business Forces U.S. Shift on Trade Treaty," by Clyde Farnsworth, *New York Times,* 23 March 1979, p. 1.

litical sensitivity of the CVD law injury test they would negotiate as a part of the subsidies code. The Executive had behind it the experience of the Kennedy Round and the failure of Congress to implement the Antidumping Code, primarily because of an injury test requiring dumped imports to be the "principal cause" of "material injury" to a domestic industry.[9]

Congress saw little reason why import competition on the basis of unfair trade practices should be tolerated. If an injury test were to be applied to the countervailing duty law, it most certainly would not be stringent. Indeed, in offering guidance about dumped imports, the Congress said that the relationship between injury to an industry and dumped imports need not be strongly causal. In fact, such imports may be only one factor contributing to injury and still provide basis for relief under unfair trade practice statutes. In the application of laws to counteract unfair trade practices, the Congress tilts toward the interests of domestic producers whose products compete with subsidized or dumped imports.[10]

Negotiators also had the benefit of advice from private advisers, whose expressions of concern throughout the process

---

[9]Richard R. Rivers and John D. Greenwald, "The Negotiation of a Code on Subsidies and Countervailing Measures: Bridging Fundamental Policy Differences," *Law and Policy in International Business* 11 (1979):1447–95. The explanation in the text is drawn largely from this article.

[10]The Senate Finance Committee report on the Trade Reform Act of 1974 [later passed as the Trade Act of 1974] states: "Moreover, the law does not contemplate that injury from less-than-fair-value imports be weighed against other factors which may be contributing to injury to an industry. The words 'by reason of' express a causation link but do not mean that dumped imports must be a [or the] principal cause, a [or the] major cause, or a [or the] substantial cause of injury caused by all factors contributing to overall injury to an industry.

"In short the Committee does not view injury caused by unfair competition, such as dumping, to require as strong a causation link to imports as would be required for determining the existence of injury under fair trade conditions."

It is also in this section of the Finance Committee report that unusual language is used to distinguish material from immaterial injury: "Obviously, the law will not recognize trifling, immaterial, insignificant or inconsequential injury. *Immaterial injury connotes spiritual injury, which may exist inside of persons not industries*" [emphasis added].

U.S. Senate, Committee on Finance, *Trade Reform Act of 1974*, p. 180.

were a reminder of the sensitivity of the issue, and a sounding board for what might be domestically acceptable.

As noted earlier, once the United States had agreed to add an injury test to its countervailing duty law, the key issue became *how* injury would be defined, as well as the relationship of injury to import competition.

Injury to industry is investigated and determined by the International Trade Commission, an independent six-person body. The commission investigates and determines injury for "escape clause" or "201" cases, and also for unfair trade practice cases. In the latter instance, the Commerce Department determines whether an unfair trade practice such as dumping or subsidizing has occurred, and the ITC determines whether injury to domestic industry exists. Prior to the passage of the Trade Agreements Act of 1979, the Treasury Department had responsibility for investigating dumping and countervailing duty cases.

In investigating injury, the commission must determine whether injury has occurred and the relationship of that occurrence to imports. There are different standards for both of these factors depending on the type of import competition. The causation principle expresses the linkage that must be shown between import competition and injury. The stricter the causation requirement, the more difficult it is to prove. A similar relationship exists with respect to injury. For both causation and injury, U.S. producers tend to favor more minimal standards.

For "escape clause" cases, which involve import competition that is fair but nevertheless disruptive, "serious" injury or the threat of serious injury must be present, and increased imports must have been, or be, the "imminent," "substantial" cause. For unfair trade practices cases, the standards are less stringent; "material" injury must be found, and imports must be a "significant" cause.

There are no hard and fast definitions governing these terms or the determination of injury due to imports. The existence of the causation principle is a recognition that injury may result for reasons other than imports. At the same time the causation standard must be framed in such a way as not to preclude a positive determination. The legislative history is instructive in this regard. In the Trade Expansion Act of 1962, the Congress approved an administration proposal to link injury explicitly with tariff concessions negotiated as part of the trade agreements program. From that time until the injury test was rewritten in the Trade Act of 1974, virtually no affirmative findings of injury were made by the International Trade Commission.

In investigating the health of a domestic industry for purposes of escape clause cases, the ITC gathers data covering a three-to-five-year period. The commission looks at information on domestic production and shipments, on the size of inventories, employment, work-hours and wages, profit or loss, prices, and trends in capacity and utilization. Information is gathered largely through questionnaires to domestic producers, to importers and to customers (especially with respect to unfair trade practices cases). Section 201 of the Trade Act of 1974, which deals with these investigations, states that in examining this information and making its determination on injury, the commission "should take into account the significant idling of productive facilities in the industry, the inability of a significant number of firms to operate at a reasonable level of profit, and significant employment or underemployment in the industry."[11] Determining what is significant and what is reasonable is a judgment call of the commission.

In investigating dumping and countervailing duty cases, the commission takes the above factors into account, and in particular pays close attention to pricing data. This is because both these unfair trade practices have to do with selling goods at artificially low prices. Thus, the commission is interested in the pricing behavior of the domestic articles with which the imports compete. The commission surveys the purchasers of both the domestic goods and the imports to determine if sales are being

---

[11]Ibid., p. 121.

lost to the imports, and if so whether a primary reason for transferring from a domestic to a foreign supplier is that of lower cost.

Although officials were not suggesting that the injury test to be added to the countervailing duty law be one requiring that "serious" injury exist, a debate over the question of "material injury" versus the even less stringent "injury" did develop.

With respect to causation, U.S. trading partners agreed that a "principal cause" formulation would prove impossible to meet and the causation standard agreed to was very close to that in the existing U.S. antidumping law. "The issue of 'material injury' versus 'injury' proved more contentious. The United States resisted inclusion of the word 'material' for some time but eventually conceded the point after an acceptable list of criteria for determining and interpreting 'material injury' had been developed and agreed to."[12]

The definition of injury ran into some opposition in Congress, and how the implementing legislation would define injury became one of the more publicly disputed issues in an otherwise uneventful—at least to the public eye—legislative process. The code's injury test had been negotiated in "close consultation with and with the support of, private sector advisers. . . . However, when it came to including in the law reference to 'material' injury, old fears were resurrected."[13] This fear was especially prevalent in the steel industry, and the industry pressed its views throughout the period of congressional consideration.[14] The industry had wide support in Congress. In the Senate, H. John Heinz III, a member of the Senate Finance Subcommittee on International Trade and a leader of the Steel Caucus, introduced two bills of interest to the industry. One, the Buy American Act of

---

[12]Rivers and Greenwald, "Negotiation of a Code on Subsidies."

[13]Ibid., p. 1491.

[14]See M. Maxwell Glen, "Negotiating the Trade Pact at Home and Abroad," *National Journal* 11 (17 March 1979):429–32. Also, various interviews with participants.

1979, would have had an impact on the government procurement code. The other bill would have amended the countervailing duty law to "make it relatively easy to prove injury, although not as easy as the steel industry favors...."[15]

The House resolved the dispute in its version of the MTN implementing legislation when on April 23 the Ways and Means Committee announced that it had voted to require the injury test to be based on material rather than minimal injury.[16] The Senate, however, had deleted the word "material" from its "bill." The issue was resolved in the "nonconference" between the two houses. "The eventual compromise, that 'the term "material injury" means harm which is not inconsequential, immaterial or unimportant,' was agreed to only after some spirited opposition by some members of the Senate Finance Committee."[17] The compromise language was midway between those who wanted "material" deleted altogether, and those, including U.S. trading partners, who wanted its inclusion along with a positive definition.

Another set of issues having to do with the countervailing duty law concerned its administration. During the 1970s there was increasing criticism from domestic producers about the government's enforcement of unfair trade laws. The "trigger price mechanism" scheme had been developed to address concerns about dumped steel imports, but there remained a widespread belief that the U.S. response to unfair trading practices was too little, too late. The issue had been raised by private sector advisers during the course of the negotiation: "Shortly after the subsidies/countervailing measures negotiation began in earnest, it became clear that private sector willingness to accept an injury test in the countervailing duty law was, among other things, conditional upon changes in countervailing duty law procedures

---

[15]Ibid., p. 431.

[16]Clyde Farnsworth, "House Unit Sets Import Injury Rule; Version Conflicts with Senate's," *New York Times,* 24 April 1979, p. 3.

[17]Rivers and Greenwald, "Negotiation of a Code on Subsidies," p. 1492.

that would better provide effective and expeditious relief.... "[18] In the international negotiations, one goal of the U.S. was to write a code that would allow flexibility during the course of the legislative process to change and tighten the administration of U.S. laws. Such changes were subsequently written into the Trade Agreements Act of 1979. Timetables were shortened, provisional duties allowed, and negotiated settlements were allowed to include price or quantity guarantees.

These changes had been designed for and largely by U.S. domestic producers. Two other groups also very involved in international trade, importers and retailers, opposed the provisions. Since their goal is to seek the widest possible import selection at the most competitive prices, they did not share the perspective that expediting the procedures of unfair trade laws was necessarily in the best economic interests of the country. Shorter timetables for investigations, they argued, would tend to give domestic industry an advantage and lead to findings of injury that might not be warranted. Importers were also opposed to provisional duties.

The importers were not able to influence members of Congress sufficiently to change the proposed procedures for unfair trade practice laws. They complained that the closed-door congressional-administration sessions hampered their ability to know what was happening to influence decisions.[19] One congressional perspective was that most domestic interests did not realize the significance of the period of congressional-executive consultations (particularly between January and March) and that they did not, for the most part, take the "trouble to get the information, formulate some ideas and then come up and talk." "The liberal trade community," another aide said, "did not make their voices felt as they should have. They didn't come up and talk to

---

[18]Ibid., p. 1490.

[19]See Clyde Farnsworth, "Pressure Mounting on Trade Packagers: Lobbyists Pursue Special Waivers; Deadline Nears," *New York Times*, 25 March 1979, Section III, p. 1.

the members. Until it was too late, they put all of their eggs in one basket of talking to the administration."

In addition to the fact that interest groups did not have ready access to the substance of discussions was the fact that expert members of Congress and their staffs had—and had had throughout the negotiation—access to all important information. They had no need to rely on information usually developed and provided by lobbyists. Moreover, they kept confidential the extent of the information they had, both because it was classified and because "we didn't want a line of people at our door."[20] Members and staff also knew that the trade agreements had been negotiated with the ongoing advice of the private sector. These factors combined to shift the dynamics of the legislative process. Just as the private sector had confidence that its representations were being taken into account by STR, the committees in this phase of the process continued to be allied with STR. The MTN process was a paradox in this regard: the process that had been imposed on, and then accepted by, the administration can be seen as weakening the control of the Executive, yet the lines of communication, domestically, were essentially bilateral and always involved the Executive, suggesting a large degree of control.

In addition to making changes in procedures for administering U.S. trade laws, the Trade Agreements Act made changes in adminstrative bodies. Throughout the period of congressional consideration, administration officials, public witnesses, and private sector advisers stressed that the test of the trade agreements would be in their implementation. The Treasury Department, which implemented antidumping and countervailing duty laws, was often criticized for inadequate enforcement. Many believed that the U.S. government was inadequately organized for trade functions, and that more aggressive trade expansion activities should be undertaken.

---

[20]Various interviews with participants.

These sentiments combined to make a presidential proposal for trade function reorganization one of the conditions for final action on the implementing legislation. The Senate Finance Committee took the lead on the issue. Senator William Roth, in particular, who served on both the Subcommittee on International Trade and the Governmental Affairs Committee,[21] was interested in reorganization. He had the support of Senator Abraham Ribicoff, chairman of the International Trade Subcommittee and member of the Governmental Affairs Committee.

Senator Roth was in favor of the creation of a Department of International Trade and Industry. The administration opposed a new department, but agreed to a reorganization. The proposal was due to be delivered to the Senate on July 10.

That deadline slipped. Robert Strauss, testifying before the International Trade Subcommittee on July 10, asked the committee to accept his personal guarantee that a plan would be delivered to the committee,[22] and to allow the bill to move forward. Although the committee refused, it was more a matter of sending a message to the bureaucracy[23] than it was a chastisement of Strauss. The administration did within the following two

---

[21]The Governmental Affairs Committee had jurisdiction over executive branch reorganization functions. As with the textile and countervailing duty waiver issues, government reorganization and passage of the MTN implementing legislation were technically separate. They were directly related politically, as the Finance Committee would not report the MTN bill until the Senate had in hand a reorganization proposal endorsed by the president.

[22]U.S. Senate, Committee on Finance, Subcommittee on International Trade, *Hearings on S 1376* (1 of 2), 10 July 1979, pp. 390–96.

[23]In his opening remarks, Senator Ribicoff said: "The problem with this trade reorganization has been the inability to tell off the various bureaucracies who keep fighting for their own piece of turf, and that continuous fighting ... prevents this Government from moving on issue after issue." Ibid., p. 394.

weeks submit a reorganization plan[24] to the Senate, and the Senate passed the MTN implementing legislation on July 23, 1979.

---

[24]The major provisions of the plan (Reorganization Plan No. 3 of 1979, implemented by Executive Order 12188, 4 January 1980) assigned overall responsibility for developing and coordinating U.S. trade policy to the Office of the U.S. Trade Representative (the name of the office was changed from Special Trade Representative to United States Trade Representative in the MTN implementing legislation); assigned administrative responsibility for most trade programs to the Commerce Department; and transferred responsibility for administering CVD and antidumping laws from the Treasury to the Commerce Department.

It was this last provision that caused the most concern in the "liberal trade community." The concern was that the Commerce Department which has historically served as an advocate of domestic industry would not bring a sufficiently internationalist perspective to the administration of these sensitive laws.

7

Assessing the Process

W AS THE TOKYO ROUND A "SUCCESS"? In what ways was it successful? What factors can be identified as contributing to the acceptance of an international agreement in its negotiated form? Is this an experiment worth repeating? Can it be repeated? Can the processes of private sector and congressional consultation be substantially applied to other types of negotiations?

The Tokyo Round of trade negotiations is widely regarded as a success in two important ways: internationally, agreements were produced, and domestically, those agreements were accepted by the United States Congress. Neither of these events was a foregone conclusion. The international negotiations had gotten off to a sluggish start, and the economic environment against which the negotiation occurred was difficult. At various points, governments considered taking a "mini-harvest"—a modest tariff reduction, for instance—and concluding. When Ambassador Strauss took office, his strategy was to "up the ante," to put more and more on the table, so that others were hesitant to walk away.

His strategy with Congress also contained that element: In explaining the agreements and testifying before Congress, Strauss stressed that the agreements would give the United States ammunition with which to combat others' unfair trade practices.

Moreover, by developing and implementing the procedures for its participation in the negotiation and consideration of the results, Congress had invested in the process, making it more difficult for the Congress to reject what those procedures had wrought. Dialogue with members of Congress provided the opportunity for Congress to give the Executive guidance on political acceptability. It provided the Executive the opportunity to educate members on negotiating requirements.

Whether the substance of the international agreements constituted a success is less clear. At the time of its passage many of those who testified before Congress adopted a wait-and-see attitude, saying that the real test of the results, especially of the nontariff barrier codes, would be after their implementation. Five years after the Round's conclusion, there is agreement that "on balance" the Tokyo Round had a modest positive effect on trade: the customs valuation code is one that is seen to have been positive, but the subsidies code has been of little use to domestic interests. The government procurement code brought "sunshine" to bidding procedures, but the list of exclusions of government entities is long.

The agreements were discrete documents; some countries entered some of them but not others. A country that has not entered an agreement does not assume its obligations, but neither does it receive its benefits. There is some concern that this will lead to a fractured system of trade rules. The Tokyo Round was not particularly successful in achieving its stated goal of bringing developing countries into the trading system.

Nevertheless, the negotiation continued a trade-liberalizing *process.* For trade negotiators this was perhaps the most important "result" of all; there was no breakdown in the international trade structure and continuity.

Thus, from a political point of view, the Tokyo Round was an outstanding success. Internationally and domestically protectionism was kept at bay. From the point of view of the executive branch of the U.S. government, the round was successful because what the Executive negotiated, the Congress implemented. From the congressional viewpoint, it was successful because Congress was kept actively informed throughout the period of negotiation and retained control over the implementing legislation. For the jurisdictional committees within the Congress, House Ways and Means and Senate Finance, it was a success because the committees had what, by 1979, was an unusual degree of control over the implementing bill. And for the U.S. private sector, it was a success because domestic interests were brought into close contact with the negotiating process.

The margin of success, 395–7 in the House, 90–4 in the Senate, is often cited as indicative of a "legislative marvel." But by the time the trade bill was on the floor of each house, it was almost a nonevent. The bill was nonamendable; differences between the House and Senate committees had been resolved some six weeks before the House floor vote. The question was whether to accept or reject. For this the provisions of the 1974 Trade Act and the procedures that had been developed by the Finance Committee for dealing with the Trade Agreements Act of 1979 can be credited. The Trade Act of 1974 insulated the bill from the "Christmas tree" amendments trade bills so often tempt.

The Finance Committee procedures, in a sense, reinstated the bill in the legislative process. That is to say, while there were differences in the sequence of events in congressional consideration, the main elements of the legislative process were present. This allowed both the appearance and the fact of significant congressional influence in executive-congressional sessions, and a large measure of control over the bill drafting itself. In Congress, the process was opened, as is normally the case, to members who had an interest in the trade legislation because of committees on which they served. In this way, a major problem with small and minority business set-asides, the only major problem, surfaced and was corrected. An aspect of the legislative process that these special procedures did not easily accommodate was the holding of public hearings.

The experience of executive-congressional and private sector cooperation in the Tokyo Round evolved from previous experiences. It also grew out of the Constitution, which guarantees Congress a role in the making of trade policy. The institution was not new to the trade field; indeed before the practice of negotiating tariffs came into being, Congress literally set the tariff rate on every item subject to taxation. For some thirty years following the debacle of the Smoot-Hawley tariff act, the executive branch was preeminent in trade matters. In the Trade Expansion Act of 1962, Congress provided for congressional advisers to negotiations, strengthened the congressional voice in escape clause proceedings, and urged the appointment of a Special Trade Representative. Even though the Nixon administration in its 1973 bill failed to allow for congressional advisers to what was then being thought of as the "Nixon Round," Congress not only reinstated advisers, but gave them official accreditation to the U.S. delegation, and in general increased the congressional role. The Trade Act of 1974 can be seen as ushering in a period (which may have been specific to the Tokyo Round) of executive-congressional cooperation.

The "sleeper" benefit of the MTN process was the private sector advisory process. While there had been good-faith efforts within the Executive to devise a system that would meet the concerns of the private sector and their supporters on Capitol Hill, there were also doubts about its usefulness for the substance of the negotiation.

The advisory process contributed positively to the substance of the negotiation. Private sector advisers told the government on what manufactures and agricultural products to seek tariff reductions. On nontariff measures, private sector advice indicated those areas in codes that needed to be flexible enough to allow changes in U.S. administrative procedure and still be in compliance with the code. It was the code negotiation on government procurement, which did not have the benefit of advice from a constituency it would affect, that had to be renegotiated.

The success of the advisory system has been credited to the ability to operate confidentially due to waiver of public meeting laws; the accountability mechanisms written into the law; and the appointment of members irrespective of party affiliation. (One participant did however criticize the Carter administration for adding affirmative action criteria for selection of committee members.)

A strong Office of the Special Trade Representative was indispensable. Congress had created the office with the objective of having it be responsive to domestic and international concerns. It was the point of origin for domestic and international negotiations. The office also managed the interagency policy process. There exists varying opinion about that process. Some say that it worked well and that through it U.S. positions in the negotiation were developed. They point to the fact that the highest-ranking tier of the interagency structure met relatively rarely to resolve matters that could not be resolved at lower levels. Others suggest that because of turf battles the interagency structure was not able to develop instructions of much use to negotiators in Geneva. Finally, opinion exists that trade policy has suffered because of weak State Department participation.

When the question is asked, "What was the single most important factor making possible the negotiation and implementation of the Tokyo Round and its agreements?" the answer is "Robert Strauss." Strauss the politician was indispensable to the process. He was able to move the negotiation forward with political solutions to substantive stalemates. While not knowledgeable about trade matters himself, he made good use of a staff that was. He maintained excellent relations with Capitol Hill. The Carter administration was not known for the smoothness of its relations with members of Congress. Strauss was, therefore, especially welcomed on the Hill.

Strauss had proximity to and the confidence of the president. He has said: "Everyone within the administration knew that Carter wanted this trade bill, that he relied on me and that I could talk to him. [They knew that] I could set trade policy, and we almost [did] set trade policy. We had the Treasury, State and

Commerce Departments—we dominated them in this field."[1]
This direction setting by the president was an important factor in
how the interagency process worked.

Strauss also benefitted from timing that worked in his favor.
While the talks in Geneva were stalled when Strauss took office,
they would either move forward or negotiators would conclude
that an agreement was not possible. U.S. negotiating authority
was running out and the talks could not legislatively span
another administration. The administration was also facing
stalemate on the countervailing duties issue with the European
Community. It was important that an agreement be reached on
this sensitive item; although framed in economic terms, it was
largely a political issue. Successive U.S. administrations had
been reluctant to impose countervailing duties on the goods of
allies, especially when there was no test required to determine if
injury were being caused. What was ultimately negotiated on
subsidies was in fact a "political" agreement negotiated out of
Washington and not Geneva.

Strauss used his political skill to create support for passage of
the implementing legislation. He loudly warned that the battle
over the trade bill would make that over the energy bill look like
a skirmish, and then quietly set about making sure that it would
not. Thus, for instance, while the United States conceded to the
European Community an increase in cheese quotas, it also
placed under quota cheeses that had not previously been subject
to quota.[2] Strauss was not concerned about the *degree* of enthusiasm for the agreements. Alonzo McDonald has said that, at
the time, few people realized that many of the "yes" votes in the
Congress were so close to "no" or to "who cares" that under other

---

[1]Interview with Robert Strauss.

[2]Dairy interests had been involved in working out an arrangement acceptable to them
but with the given that cheese quotas would be increased. They continued, however, to
press their case against quota expansion to the Congress.

circumstances a head count would have designated them swing votes.[3] Even the AFL–CIO was passive about the trade bill.

Strauss had not received the support of some interests, such as the textile industry and textile labor unions, without giving something in return. The textile package announced in early 1979 was one domestic "concession" that some in the administration and in the private sector criticized as being too high a price to pay. Previously, Strauss had negotiated Orderly Marketing Agreements limiting imports of nonrubber footwear and color television sets. In 1979, President Carter reversed his decision of the year before and granted import relief to the U.S. bolt, nut and screw industry. On the export side of trade, the Carter administration developed an export promotion plan, and the Commerce Department began conducting well-publicized trade missions.

Making concessions to domestic interests was not peculiar to this negotiation; it was business as usual, especially with respect to textiles. The industry had received special notice at the time the Trade Expansion Act was under consideration in the early 1960s. Part of that special notice led to the negotiation of the Long-Term Agreement on cotton textiles, which later evolved into the Multi-Fiber Agreement.

Adjustment assistance, also seen at times as a "payment" for the pursuit of liberal trade policies, had been introduced in 1962 and strengthened in 1974. Very little aid was given in the period between 1962 and 1974, largely because of the strict injury causation requirements of the program. These requirements were relaxed in the Trade Act of 1974, as were the requirements for the granting of import relief. Although adjustment assistance was the preferred response of the Williams Commission and the liberal trade establishment to injury due to import competition, politically it was not a viable option. The U.S. economy in the 1970s was not very resilient. Patterns of trade had changed and

[3]Interview with Alonzo McDonald.

the U.S. was suffering trade deficits rather than enjoying trade surpluses. The mood was to attempt to stop a deterioration, rather than to "pay off" workers and businesses.

The key factor in avoiding the formation of opposing coalitions to the trade agreements may well have come as a result of an institutional act rather than an individual's actions. Private sector advisers were much closer to the negotiating process than they had been in the past. On a regular basis they were told what was happening and why. This communication during the period of negotiation ameliorated pressure for changes in the agreements after the negotiation had been concluded.

As the United States prepares for another round of trade negotiations, the question arises of whether the political success of the MTN can be repeated. The Trade Agreements Act of 1979 extended for eight years the authority of the president to enter trade negotiations. The legislative procedure of the Trade Act of 1974 would govern the consideration of new agreements. The 1979 act also extended the life of the advisory committee structure. The system would certainly be called into play for a new negotiation. Many people believe, however, that the system has been weakened and trade expertise diminished by the Reagan administration's politicization of committee membership.

From time to time, the continued existence of the Office of the United States Trade Representative is called into question. Support periodically surfaces for the creation of a Department of International Trade and Industry. In 1984 the Executive endorsed this congressional initiative, but with no visible results, as in the past. Even if such a consolidation were to occur, the function if not the office and title of the U.S. Trade Representative would remain. There is a need for synthesis of trade issues into a coherent policy, and this can be done effectively only by such an office as the USTR.

Given the increasing congressional role—some say incursion—in the foreign policymaking process, there is the question of whether the practices used in the Tokyo Round could be applied successfully to other international negotiations, especially those for which congressional implementation of the results is needed.[4]

The Tokyo Round negotiations succeeded, at least, in reaching a conclusion and obtaining a broad consensus in Congress at the same time as other major negotiations involving the United States were in serious difficulty: the Panama Canal Treaties, SALT II, and the Law of the Sea.

There were similarities. Each also employed a special negotiator appointed by the President. There were consultations with the Congress and efforts by the administration, at least in the cases of the Panama Canal Treaties and SALT, to reach domestic constituencies in order to solicit understanding and support. But, in contrast to the Tokyo Round, the Panama Canal Treaties obtained congressional concurrence only after a bitter fight and extensive further negotiations with Panama. SALT II was never ratified and was subsequently withdrawn. Despite eight years of negotiating the Law of the Sea Treaty there was, even under President Carter, doubt that it could be ratified.

What was different about the Tokyo Round? Are there any lessons to be drawn that can be applied to different kinds of negotiations?

The Multilateral Trade Negotiations never became a partisan matter. While personnel changed, there were no sharp switches in the approach to the issue such as occurred in the SALT II negotiations.

Clear responsibility for the negotiation was established in the Office of the Special Trade Representative. There were relatively fewer opportunities for other parts of the Executive to affect the negotiations or state differing public views. There was, similarly, in the Congress a recognized focus of responsibility in the primary jurisdictional committees.

Perhaps even more important in assessing the differences is the fact that, in a trade or economic negotiation, there is a

---

[4]See Robert C. Cassidy, "Negotiating on Negotiations," pp. 279–80.

definable constituency that can be mobilized for consultation. While there may be broader public attitudes, the views of the industries and economic elements directly affected prevail. Economic negotiations do not, in most cases, face the disparate, often divided and frequently ill-informed groups that form the disputing constituencies of a political negotiation. Because these constituencies are difficult to define precisely, it is correspondingly difficult to create the kind of consultative mechanism that existed with the private sector in the Tokyo Round.

Congressional attention is more narrowly focussed and under the extensive influence of the Ways and Means and Finance committees. It is unlikely that such control would be ceded on highly political matters. A member of Congress also has a greater problem in defining precisely how to deal with the conflicting views within his district on a political matter than with the more precise issues and constituencies of trade.

Perhaps there is little that is transferable in the experience of a trade negotiation to the diplomacy of arms control and bilateral political relations. If there is, it lies in the effective integration of congressional and diplomatic actions demonstrated during the Tokyo Round. In the adversarial atmosphere that frequently surrounds political issues, this has seldom been tried. But, as experience of the last decade and a half has demonstrated, such integration is essential if the results of U.S. diplomacy are to receive the national acceptance necessary for effective international agreements.

Appendix

As Dick Rivers has said, much of the story of the Tokyo Round is anecdotal. The following are excerpts from interviews with some of the participants in the trade negotiation. By and large, these remarks do not include the interviewer's questions.

Interview with Robert S. Strauss

Robert S. Strauss was the Special Trade Representative from 1977 to 1979. The success of the Tokyo Round is widely credited to him. Strauss is a prominent politician in the Democratic Party and former chairman of the Democratic National Committee. He is a partner in the law firm of Akin, Gump, Strauss, Hauer and Feld. His associate, Richard Rivers, who served as general counsel in the Office of the STR when Strauss was STR, comments briefly in these excerpts.

On reviving the negotiations:

When I started this job, I didn't really know anything about the trade issues except in broad generalities, having dealt with them as a lawyer and through general readings. We spent some time getting started. As Alan Wolff, who was my deputy then, was describing the world situation to me and the domestic situation in terms of what we faced, it was pretty obvious that my political background was going to be a strong asset for me in this job. We entered on a strategy of bringing the various constituencies together that would be needed, first, to relaunch a stalled set of international negotiations and, second, and at the same time, redeveloping a political strategy to get it through the Congress: first to attract the attention of the American public, and second to convince them that this was not in the worst but in the best interest of this country. The idea then was to use that constituency to get it through the Congress.

I think as I look back, one of the most important things I did was early in the game. One of the first statements I made was in New York. I made a speech in which I said that agriculture was going to be put on the front burner and not on the back burner as it had been in previous negotiations. Within a few weeks after my appointment and that speech, the agricultural interests came in to see me with great concern and considerable negative attitudes. The first thing I remember pointing out to the head of that delegation was that I had gone to New York and in a very unlikely place made a strong statement about where agriculture belonged in these negotiations. I said that in the past our negotiators slipped out to Kansas and whispered to a few people that agriculture was important; they didn't walk into Wall Street where people thought it should only be industrial. So that's the type of thing we did.

On relations with trading partners:

We had to first get the European Community to come to the table, so to speak, in a serious way. The Japanese are never leaders, they are followers. The Europeans were the absolute essential ingredient if this thing was going to work. I went to Brussels to talk with the Europeans. They were frightened to death where this could lead them with the problems they had—one of their great concerns was that this country was going to try to destroy the Common Agricultural Policy. I remember saying, "You have to give me your bottom line. What is it that you just cannot live with?" One of the main things they said was that an attack to detroy the CAP would present great difficulties to them, and while they wish it was not there, politically they could not get into that subject. They had one or two other subjects like that.

I told them that, for the purposes of these negotiations, "You have my word there will be no attack on common agricultural policies. Now we could try to open it, to penetrate your markets more. We have got to do that, but we are not going to attack the structure itself; we just want you to open it a bit. We will negotiate hard over it, but we will not destroy it."

Once they became relaxed on two or three of those key things they couldn't stand, they agreed to sit down. At the same time, we told them two or three things that we weren't going to let them attack. So we began to creep forward and we began to develop a personal relationship and I had very good people involved who really knew these issues.

When that started, the Japanese of course were pleased to join in.

On the overwhelming domestic acceptance of the trade agreements:

I like to think that we converted everyone at the time. We had to make many compromises, of course; we did not turn out a 99 and 44/100 percent pure negotiation. I think our negotiation was A+ and that we achieved all that was possible. It was certainly not A+ in achieving what needed to be done. There was a great deal we didn't get done in subsidies, but we got a lot done (we did nothing in the service industry because we just couldn't get to it). The basic things we had to achieve— put some rules in place—we achieved; in opening markets, we got the basic things done but not the ultimate things; and more important than any of these things, we held off strong protectionist forces—we took the wind out of their sails when it looked like this country was going protectionist. You can remember how popular John Connally's speech was about letting them sit [on the docks in Japan] in their Toyotas listening to their Sonys, and so forth and so on. He was not the only one.

The president was strongly (and President Carter deserves a great deal of credit) supportive of whatever we did. He believed in an enlightened trade policy for this country. I truthfully say he never really choked on any tough issue even though it was politically unpopular. Not only did he support me here and with the Congress, but he supported me within the administration.

Of equal importance, we had two or three summits where we had to drag the French kicking and screaming and we had to force others to do certain things; and Carter let me go into those summit meetings and raise all kinds of hell and really embarrass some of the heads of state, if you will; and we took on the French [Giscard d'Estaing] in the toughest possible way in the summit in Bonn. Carter let me do it and never backed away one inch. During that time, [FRG Chancellor] Schmidt and I developed a personal relationship; [British Prime Minister] Callahan and I developed a personal relationship. All these things stood in great stead, and during that time I developed a strong relationship with people who were handling the EEC's business. We were more than negotiators; we became personal friends.

All of these things—they were strengths of mine—made up for my lack of competence in other areas. These became people whose burdens and troubles I shared and they shared mine; and when we finally finished, I really put together a worldwide group of people who related to each other, including the Japanese. That's tough but it's important. When the day's work was over, we then would have four or five social hours and we would get all of our work done after the day's work was over. People could relax and say what they could and could not do and what they would try to do to help the other. First thing you know we had a moving negotiation and we started reaching conclusions, putting things to bed. We reached for an attainable goal and we dealt with it in a pragmatic, real-world way.

By the time we came back here, we had already done much work and continued to do much work with the constituencies. Those constituencies who at first were negative were finally calling and writing their congressmen and senators saying, "This is (or isn't) what I wanted but Bob Strauss deserves support." Lo and behold, we passed [the implementing legislation] by such a wide margin. You wouldn't believe this but when the Kennedy Round was concluded, the headline in the *Washington Post* said the single achievement of the administration will undoubtedly be the Kennedy Round; but the *Washington Post* didn't even mention that the Tokyo Round results had passed the Congress. I called and raised hell about it and they said, well, it wasn't news anymore because everyone knew what was going to happen; there was no opposition. It's a rather funny little story, evaluating the times that it didn't merit mention in the *Washington Post.* All that work, all that sweat.

On upping the ante:

We had to swap some things, we had to trade and negotiate; we had to put some things on the table. [Some were afraid the negotiation would collapse.] I kept saying, just keep more and more issues on the table and keep putting more things in the pot. The higher the bills, greed will get every participant, and they will all stay in to try to get their share of the pot. I said it's just like drawing to an inside straight in poker, if the pot's big enough you pay whatever it takes to take a shot at it. They are all afraid to walk away. Sure enough, every time they started to walk away and said they were through, they would look back and see all these goodies we put up there.

RICHARD RIVERS. It was very important internationally, in terms of sustaining the negotiations, because rather than take the minimalist result which had been proposed at one time—let's just call this a victory and go home—the U.S. pursued a policy of putting things in the pot to the point that it became realized in Tokyo, Brussels and other capitals that the risk of failure was unacceptable. It was too big an operation to allow to come to naught. They were afraid of the risk of failure so it became almost condemned to succeed.

STRAUSS. That's what made the Europeans stand up to the French. The French would never have let this go through; they would have stopped it, they didn't want it. But it just meant so much to so many, they couldn't stand the pressure, the political heat, in Europe if they had not let us go forward.

On relations with Congress:

Senator [Abraham] Ribicoff, who chaired the [Finance Committee] trade subcommittee, and Senator Russell Long (then chairman of the Finance Committee) were the two key players we needed. I convinced them that they ought to go to Geneva. They spent two days in Geneva and our staff put on a dog and pony show over there. For the first time they really saw just how far along we were and that we knew where it was going and were negotiating something worthwhile for this country. So you had Russell Long and Ribicoff in place, and they really were great stalwarts in here. They never choked a bit; they stayed with us all the way.

Bill Roth on the Republican side was equally good and he became committed to this. I spent a lot of time talking to him. So I had the Senate in good shape there.

We had a chairman of the House Ways and Means Committee Trade Subcommittee who was committed to this anyway [Rep. Charles Vanik of Ohio]. He was good and helpful. We not only needed these people for the Tokyo Round, but we had other trade issues coming up every day that we would have to deal with in pragmatic ways. If it wasn't on television it was on shoes; if it wasn't on shoes it was mushrooms; if it wasn't mushrooms it was on steel. It ran the gamut.

I also stayed in very close touch with the Republican side. Barber Conable was a strong supporter as was [William] Frenzel from Minnesota. And I was in touch not only with our [Democratic] leadership but with the leadership on the Republican side. I met with John Rhodes and others. When I finished he stood up and said, "Well, go back and worry about your Democrats. We'll deliver a higher percentage of votes than the Democrats do." Everybody clapped and cheered a little, so they were supportive.

That came from many hours on the Hill just sitting talking about what the problems were. You had to talk to the steel caucus. They had terrible problems and we worked with them every day, and I really mean that, literally every day. I didn't every day, but every couple of weeks I would be with someone. The same thing with people who were interested in specialty crops in California. I went to California and explained to those farmers especially what we were trying to do, whether it was in raisins or in citrus. The first thing you know they were sending word back to their people. In Florida we had constant meetings on citrus again down there. The New York congressional delegation would come in here and have their weekly meeting. Once in a while I met with them, answering their questions, and they all had questions. They all understood it as we went along. I frankly think this kind of effort was unprecedented, not only in trade but in other fields.

On the lack of attention—especially negative attention—from the general public:

It should have been far more violent than the others [e.g., SALT II, Panama Canal], because it really dealt with the bone issues when you start talking about the income of farmers, and imports and exports that affect major industries and major companies. Labor violently opposed freer trade policy. We just kept in touch with people, had meetings with the Business Roundtable, with the business councils, and individual labor people.

RIVERS. I recall in the middle of the Carter administration there was a story in the *Washington Post* in which some unidentified young White House official said that the difference between SALT and the MTN package was that the MTN package was an inside-the-beltway [the highway circling Washington, D.C.] issue and that SALT was an outside-the-beltway issue, and I thought to myself at the time, well, they have got it exactly wrong. We had successfully camouflaged it. It was SALT that was inside-the-beltway, and it was the MTN that was outside—potentially the more bitter national debate.

STRAUSS. If you go back and look at my travel schedule, it was Illinois and South Dakota, it was Sacramento and it was Salt Lake City, and in and out of Chicago to get that market, and in and out of Florida to get the southeast, and in and out of Atlanta to get the southeast. We saved Boston till later on until we could give them something there.

And then we had a great problem. We had to give up some things, for example, in alcohol [e.g., wine gallon/proof gallon]. We really had to trade off. And it could have been the most bitter issue of all. But still, interestingly enough, the Kentucky [congressional] delegation stayed with us, because we showed what we were getting for them. What we did on that was, we put real heat on tobacco and other things, so that when we took [liquor protection] away, we still had a constituency in Kentucky and through these states. So that enabled people like Wendell Ford [from Kentucky], who wanted to help us, to be able politically to survive. Can you imagine a Louisville, Kentucky senator voting against the liquor industry? Well he did and survived. And we told the liquor industry that we were trading some of you away toward the larger good and that we had to put something on the table.

Interview with
Frederick L. Montgomery

Frederick L. Montgomery is Deputy U.S. Assistant Trade Repre-
sentative. During the Tokyo Round he was the director of the Office of
International Trade Policy of the Department of Commerce. That
office was responsible for the Commerce Department's input in the
interagency process that developed U.S. positions for the trade
negotiations. The office was also responsible for the management of
the industry private sector advisory process. Mr. Montgomery was
asked largely about the private sector advisory process and its relation
to government decision making.

On the operations of the private advisory committees:

That was quite an extensive process. The industry advisory program, which was co-chaired with the USTR but administered principally by the Department of Commerce, was organized along sectoral lines. We had some two dozen industry sector advisory committees, or ISACs, for various sectors of industry: chemicals, nonferrous metals, etc. In addition, we had an Industry Policy Advisory Committee, which was made up of about a dozen or so individuals at the Chief Executive Officer (CEO) level. It was a group that operated and met less frequently and whose purpose was to provide policy-level advice from an industry perspective for the negotiation. There were these two tiers, but the principal work on a day-to-day basis was with the two dozen or so ISACs.

What we did—by the way, the number of people involved here was in the neighborhood of five hundred advisers, quite a large number of people to work with systematically—was to eventually adopt a formula to have each of the committees, ISACs, participate in what we called a "round of meetings" and we would have two or three of these rounds a year. We would take a period of time over about three-to-five weeks and have each of the committees meet during that period. We usually would prepare for them a common agenda of issues which we needed to go over that were the issues involved in the negotiation. In addition, we would have specific topics that we wanted to take that were of concern to a particular committee.

What we attempted to do was to identify the issues where we needed private sector input, meet with them, try to get their views on them, and then, in turn, feed that into the interagency decision-making process. From time to time, instead of meeting in individual committees, we would hold what we call plenary sessions on a particular issue or issues in which we wanted to brief the entire group on where things stood in negotiations or to talk about some particular topic. We would hold those in the auditorium over at Commerce, and we'd hold the plenary session maybe two or three times a year.

In addition, as time went by we felt the need for quicker turnaround. We put together a group of ISAC chairmen and that allowed us to deal more quickly, more comprehensively with about two dozen people in shorter, smaller sessions. That became by the end of negotiation a favorite instrument to use, particularly when we needed to get a reaction rather quickly to something. Then we could pick up the details with the individual committees, if necessary, later on. This was a system that had not existed previous to the Tokyo Round; it was created in the '74 Trade Act. So it was the first time out with it, and it naturally tended to evolve over a period of time. By the time we got to the end of negotiations we had something like three groups with which we were working, depending upon the situation: either the individual committees, or the ISAC chairmen's group, or the IPAC, the Industry Policy Advisory Committee.

At any rate, this information and advice would then be collected and written up by the staff at Commerce and would be fed into the interagency process. It was understood, right from the beginning—in fact, this is in the Trade Act—that the information and advice obtained from the private sector was just that. In other words, this would not be automatically accepted but, rather, was to be seen as a tool for the government to use. What we would do is to provide the interagency group with the advice that ISACs had provided, but separately we would indicate the position of the Department of Commerce. Sometimes those two coincided and sometimes they didn't. We're talking here about a large number of issues and, of course, with a lot of nuances to them as the negotiations developed. So, there were perhaps two tracks: we wanted to make sure—this was very important to the advisers—that their advice was actually made available to the inter-agency process. That, however, we saw as a separate matter from the position taken on any particular issue by the Department of Commerce. That was really a judgment of a government agency.

We tried, to the extent possible, to make sure that when the Trade Policy Staff Committee [TPSC] took a decision on any particular issue, it knew what the views of the private sector were on that issue, and that it knew from the advisory committee's point of view. That would be true not only of industry but of agriculture as well. It should be noted that the TPSC is the first level in the interagency decision-making process where members can in effect sign off for their agencies and have an agreed administration position. The levels above that were more in the nature of the appeal levels; but if it got through the TPSC, that, in effect, was administration policy. So, it was very important that by the time we actually got to the TPSC discussion or decision, we had the information from the private sector as part of the input to decisions taken.

On staffing responsibilities and Commerce/STR joint administration:

Each committee was assigned a "designated federal officer" from the Commerce Department. In USTR there was also a staff member assigned to follow each of the committees; this wasn't just for the industry committee but also the agriculture and labor committees. This person didn't have the status under the law that the person in Commerce did, but that was more a technicality than anything else. As a matter of fact, they came to be referred to as the "godparents." Each committee had a godparent in USTR, but it was done on a more informal basis because Commerce was still basically administering the industry program. The godparents' role tended to come into play when there was an actual meeting, after which they would back off a little bit in the periods in between.

In Commerce we were much more concerned with the day-to-day contacts and the handling of the information flow. There was an enormous amount of paper that went back and forth, what with getting a piece of paper out to the ISAC, getting reactions back from them—that secretarial function was by and large performed by Commerce. However, when the committees met, in addition to the designated federal official from Commerce, there would be one of the godparents from USTR who would come to the meetings. Then, in addition, depending upon what was on the agenda, the technical experts from Commerce and/or STR would come and brief the committee on that particular issue. We would shuffle people in and out of the meetings. The two contacts—the designated federal official and the godparent from USTR—let the committee members feel that they had at least one person in each place that they could deal with.

On the Industrial Policy Advisory Committee:

During the height of negotiations the IPAC met no more than two or three times a year. With ISACs, while the round meetings were about as frequent, there were, in addition, meetings of the ISAC chairmen and individual ISAC meetings that took place apart from the so-called rounds. So, again, those groups variously met more frequently than the IPAC.

The way things finally worked out was that for the eighteen or twenty members of the IPAC, each ISAC had a designated representative or contact on the IPAC. This was not a situation where the ISAC information and advice came up the line in the system and, in fact, was then delivered by the IPAC; they were separate. The IPAC tended to focus its attention on the broader issues of the negotiation, the overall direction and objectives, and did not get involved, generally, in advice on specific tariffs or nontariff barriers.

There was a lot more discussion in the IPAC on the various nontariff barrier codes: what U.S. objectives were in obtaining them, how important they were—sort of the overall thrust of the administration's policy objectives. The codes were something that was being attempted for the first time on any kind of scale in the Tokyo Round. Previous rounds have been primarily, if not exclusively, devoted to tariffs. The IPAC tended not to deal with tariffs, with occasional exceptions. Instead it tended to focus on the broader codes that we were attempting to negotiate.

On the effect of the change in administration (1976 elections):

You have to keep in mind that we went across two administrations in the Tokyo Round, and we started out in the period prior to '76 with one administration and one group of people, particularly on the IPAC. The negotiations ground down. We went through the period of U.S. elections, and in the '76 election, of course, the Carter administration came in. We clearly had a change in the U.S. negotiators. We also had a change in some of the advisers; we had to pick things up again. While there was very little change in the ISAC process and membership, there did tend to be a fairly large change in the IPAC. So we had to try to pick up new people, in a way go back to the drawing board on what this whole thing was all about.

The new administration had to identify its own objectives and priorities in the negotiations, including what our timetable was. For example, one of the issues we got into a squeeze on at the end of the negotiations was the safeguards code. It was one of the areas on which we failed to reach agreement. That issue was discussed in the IPAC. There were different negotiations involving government procurement and on subsidies that required some difficult decisions toward the end. It was in areas like that that we sought IPAC advice.

On the merits of technical and policy advice:

Certainly both types of advice are useful. I think it depends upon what the issues are that the government is facing at any particular point in time. In the beginning, and at the end, I think that you tend to rely more heavily on broader kinds of judgments—in the beginning, obviously, in developing the objectives for a round of negotiations, at the end, in trying to make a judgment as to whether you have gotten what you felt you needed to get. Those kinds of judgments which are broadly political, not in a partisan sense but in a more general sense, are best carried out at a political level of government and, again, at the higher levels in industry. In this kind of negotiation, however, where you're dealing with literally thousands of tariff lines, both in the case of the United States and with our trading partners and with specifics in those various codes, you absolutely have to have the technical level of advice. That really was the heart of the program. I didn't mention it earlier but the phase of the exercise that was probably most systematic, most comprehensive, was the tariff advice. We literally got advice on the entire tariff with respect to what our advisers felt the U.S. could offer consistent with what our legislative mandate was. And as importantly, what they thought we ought to try to obtain in foreign markets. This is literally line-by-line advice. That kind of input can only come from the technical level. I think that would be my sense of the issue.

On the Kennedy Round experience:

The private sector advisory system was developed largely as an outgrowth of dissatisfaction with the Kennedy Round. There was the feeling that the private sector in other countries had a much more regular relationship with those countries' negotiators, and that somehow or another the U.S. was at a disadvantage. We, in fact, did have input during the Kennedy Round but it was simply not as massive and certainly not as systematic as we finally developed for the purposes of the Tokyo Round.

On the success of the advisory system:

I think its success was reflected in the fact that Congress extended it in the 1979 Trade Agreements Act. I have a certain amount of personal pride in the outcome, being associated with the office [International Trade Policy] that had the responsibility for it in Commerce. I liked to say at the time, and still feel, that it's a program that can be pointed to in government that works. You constantly hear criticism of the bureaucracy and how things don't work, but this was a massive program that really did work; and I think that all the people who were involved in it really deserve the credit for making it work, both on the private side and the public side.

I feel rather strongly that the program benefits from being kept in operation. But I will be the first to admit, and it's true not only in the private sector, it's true also in the government, that when we're not involved in a major round of negotiation, there is not the same degree of interest. Unfortunately in the trade area it's one of those things that if you are not moving forward, you are very likely to be moving backward. There seems to be no middle ground.

Interview with Richard R. Rivers

Richard R. Rivers is a member of the law firm of Akin, Gump, Strauss, Hauer and Feld. He served as general counsel, Office of the Special Trade Representative, during the Tokyo Round of trade negotiations.

On the background to the Tokyo Round:

All the previous negotiations, with the exception of the Kennedy Round, had been fairly cut-and-dry. Basically in those situations the Congress had given the President authority to reduce tariffs in the context of negotiated agreements. Trade negotiators went out and basically traded tariff concession for tariff concession. As the tariffs came down, it was generally recognized that nontariff barriers were proliferating and posed at least as significant or more significant a barrier to trade—distortions in the trading system. So in the 1960s there was a lot of preparation for the Tokyo Round effort.

In the Kennedy Round there was an attempt to tackle some problems in the nontariff barrier excercise. There was the unhappy experience with the antidumping code in which many people felt that the negotiators had been disingenuous and not entirely above board with the Congress and with the private sector. And Congress felt that it had been disserved by the fact that it hadn't been adequately briefed by the executive branch and indeed that the negotiations had been conducted without private sector advice.

It was in this context that the procedures were set up in the Trade Act of 1974: the consultative procedures between the executive branch and the Congress, as well as the procedures that are unprecedented, in which Congress undertook to amend its own rules (the House and Senate rules) in order to provide for up-and-down consideration of trade agreements in implementing legislation. The entire private sector advisory system was set up.

I would say the best way to tackle the problem of understanding what happened in the Tokyo Round is not so much to go look in the archives of the dry and dusty records of those negotiating sessions. The most interesting material was probably not recorded, and it's probably in interviews such as this with participants that you will get the real flavor and essence of what happened. Part of it is almost anecdotal.

I really had a dual responsibility. I was the general counsel in the Office of the Special Trade Representative in Washington. I was based here, not directly attached to the Geneva delegation. However, the subsidies negotiation had really gone nowhere and the Geneva delegation was more than happy to wash their hands of the subsidies negotiations. John Greenwald undertook to try, beginning in early 1977, to develop a new position for the United States in these negotiations and to begin almost shuttling, initially between Washington and Brussels, to try to find some common ground and then build a web, including more and delegations, and at the same time brief key private sector advisers. Early on we involved advisers in the process, because it was recognized that we could go out and negotiate a subsidies agreement but the whole thing would be doomed unless we were able to convince 51 percent of the domestic sentiment that it was in the interest of the United States and in their particular sectoral interest that the subsidies code be adopted and that U.S. law be conformed accordingly; including an injury test, which was the basic issue in the subsidies negotiation.

The process of consultation served more than one purpose. One was that in a negotiating context you could impress upon your counterpart early on those areas in which you could give and those areas where you could not give.

JOAN TWIGGS. *How did you develop what was and was not possible to achieve?*

RIVERS. Initially you would use your own political judgment about what you thought was doable and what was beyond your grasp. What we did was shuttle back and forth and ultimately we got into the substance of the negotiation and began to circulate papers. Indeed we even leaked papers to private advisers to get their reaction. It had a profound impact. You would spend maybe ten days in Geneva of round-the-clock negotiating sessions, getting very little sleep, going around getting the feel of the Community and each of the member state delegations, the Canadians, the Indians, and all of the participating countries. You would find out a sense of what they wanted; what their objectives were; what you wanted from them.

The life of a trade negotiator, and I suspect any negotiator, is a fairly lonely life. You feel sort of trapped between two sides. You are over there in Geneva and you are engaged in a sort of hand-to-hand struggle with your counterpart going over text, bracketed language, etc., and you find out that language dropped out was wanted by someone, etc. Yes, it's a fairly lonely life. You don't have a lot of friends.

We undertook to get private advisers to accompany us to Geneva. I was very successful in involving certain private advisers in the negotiating, people who were seasoned, experienced and initially very skeptical that any kind of acceptable agreement [on subsidies] could be reached. But they were people susceptible to reason and argument and they were prepared to travel with us and listen to us and hear us out.

Others were much more suspicious or unwilling to be drawn into the process. They were to a great extent hoping the subsidies negotiations would fail. If it failed, they could withhold their support from the whole package on the grounds that it did not comprehensively deal with all of the problems of the trading system and in fact failed to deal with the most central problem afflicting the trading system—subsidies and state-owned enterprise.

In one particular industry, the steel industry, we were never able to elicit specific advice from them. We went through a process of about six months of negotiations [in Geneva]. I'll never forget that we had finally reached the point at which the first bracketed blue-band text of the GATT document was to be distributed. We had at this point expanded. Originally the negotiations were just between the U.S. and the Community, and then we brought the Canadians to the table; then we brought other developed countries to the table, the Australians; and then we expanded to include certain developing countries. Finally, we had about ten delegations participating in the drafting session. We worked up a tentative text with the outline on subsidies and countervailing duties.

I'll never forget we had one last session before that text was to be distributed, in which we were meeting with the GATT Secretariat. It was really just an editorial session; we were going over the final draft before it was turned over to the GATT Secretariat for mimeographing and distribution as a GATT blue-band document. This was really supposed to be almost an historical event, because for seven years there had never been any kind of text on subsidies circulated among delegations; no one had ever gotten that far.

That night we came back at ten after dinner to work, however long, to finish the text, and there was delivered to me a large brown envelope with the views and recommendations of the American Iron and Steel Institute. They were about a year late in arriving. I opened the package and realized what it was. I was the chairman of the group so I gaveled the meeting to order, pressed the green button and popped up the flag of the United States. I said that I had just received the advice of the American steel industry as to what ought to go into this text. I asked for a one-hour adjournment to permit me to review this text because it was very important that something of theirs find its way into this agreement. The domestic steel industry of the United States would have a large say on whether the code negotiation was successful or not. We were able to identify five things that the industry wanted that we felt we had a chance of getting into the text. I think ultimately we got all five in.

It had a tremedous impact on advisers to see a change in an internationally negotiated text that reflected their comment. It is an astonishing process. Advisers become almost coparticipants. As long as a steel executive feels that he has no impact or influence over an international negotiating process, his attitude is one of unmitigated hostility and antagonism. But the moment that text even in a minor way reflects some input by him—I don't want to overstate this, but there is a curious phenomenon—then he becomes much more interested in the process and much more willing to participate in a kind of give-and-take.

Although the steel industry never loomed large in the advice during the negotiating process, when we brought the agreements home and undertook to draw up the implementing legislation, the steel industry became critical. John Greenwald and I spent at least two or three nights a week for the better part of two months with representatives of the domestic steel industry—walking them through the agreement, ex-plaining the provisions of the code and most importantly walking them through our draft and proposals for implementing it in U.S. law. So there was a domestic negotiation with private advisers which was every bit as important as the international.

On the domestic and international climate:

In the Ford administration, Special Trade Representative Frederick Dent really had a problem in that there was no consensus internationally or even domestically here in the United States, except for the small, traditional, liberal trade community, to go forward with those negotiations. Fred Dent had the unhappy assignment of trying to push forward with something that not many people particularly cared about, and I think to some extent our trading partners wanted to wait for the presidential election. Most of them really hoped that this negotiation would go away. It was a curious situation. No single country wanted to strangle the negotiations. They didn't want the blame for having actively killed the Tokyo Round, but there were a number of them that would have been just as pleased to have it expire of its own accord—the French, in particular. You had an unhappy global economic picture: slow growth, recession, high unemployment.

Fred Dent's thought was that one way of getting some interest in this Tokyo Round was to have a so-called miniharvest. That is, let's have an initial tariff cut in order to generate some interest in trade negotiations. I could see what he had in mind. He was trying to put something on the table so people would say that maybe there is something worthwhile in this. On the other hand, people, including myself, were concerned that what would happen was that, with the notion of a miniharvest, once you started the process it would very soon dissolve and become nothing—that the miniharvest would really become a sham for winding down and terminating the Tokyo Round.

When Strauss came in (part of it was due to his own personality; he is not a person to do things on a modest scale), he had a president who was committed to the process of the liberal trading system. I don't really know how it came about but pretty soon we were not only rejecting the miniharvest, we were actively expanding the scope of the Tokyo Round. It became such a large undertaking that it was condemned to success, because the risk of failure was more than anybody could contemplate. The downside became too costly for everybody.

The Trade Act procedures were completely untested and unprecedented really. There was some concern that what we were about involved so much domestic political energy [and] some controversy, that the system really would not be able to sustain the buffeting in domestic politics that it was likely to receive. But they didn't anticipate the extent to which we were prepared, as Strauss has said, to get into bed with the Congress and with the private sector.

Under the law, for example, technically we could have brought those agreements back and drawn up a law to implement them into U.S. law—made all the conforming changes in the Internal Revenue Code, in all the other laws that were affected by the international agreement—and then walked outside and dropped the proposals in the mailbox to the Speaker of the House and the President Pro Tem [of the Senate] and set in motion a series of procedures that would have resulted in an up-or-down vote in the House or Senate. No one could stop it. We could have done that, but it would have been at great risk of ultimately losing the whole package and antagonizing the Congress.

I don't think anybody anticipated the extent to which we were prepared to go down and consult with the Congress in an informal way on developing the implementation package itself. So that by the time we undertook to drop it in the mailbox, the Congress had had a large hand and they knew what was coming down. The interesting thing is, as I was later told by some friends of mine on the Hill, that they were astonished that we hadn't tried to slip something in. We had an agreement on a draft and that draft was ultimately what President Carter submitted to the Congress.

On congressional observers and private sector advisers:

What people did in Geneva depended on the individual. Most of them met with some heads of other delegations, were briefed by the MTN delegation and talked with some of the GATT Secretariat people. They sort of got a feel for the process. But they didn't really roll up their sleeves and get into the nitty gritty, by and large. There were exceptions—members of Congress, who by reason of their constituency or their own particular interest really undertook to become knowledgeable about the negotiations generally and with some emphasis on detail; people like [the late Representative William] Steiger, [Representative William] Frenzel, people like this who could talk in an informed way about every code and the interest of almost every country there.*

---

*Both sat on the House Ways and Means Trade Subcommittee.

That process, I think, worked. It gave them a sense or feel for the negotiation that was missing in previous trade negotiations; it was certainly missing in the SALT negotiations. I recall in some of those briefings by congressional staffers there would be rather important signals and exchanges in which members of Congress would say, "Well, I can understand under the right circumstances we might be prepared to amend the law provided we can get A, B, C." Or you would get a kind of political signal from a senior member of Congress that something was doable, something you might not have thought was doable. I know that happened in the subsidies and countervailing area. We sat down, Bob Strauss and I and others, and briefed [Senators] Russell Long, Abe Ribicoff and others on the whole question of border taxes and the rebate of indirect taxes. Many people were saying that they wanted a change in the rules. That was simply beyond reach with respect to the rebate of indirect taxes; and if you wanted to pull the plug on the negotiations, that would be a good issue to do it. Basically, we told those senators we can't do that, but we can do this, this and this.

An interesting aspect that I frequently have to impress upon people was that private sector advisers were not there as representatives of their particular companies. In fact, the law provided a penalty if they were to share negotiating information with their own companies. They were there because of their individual expertise as private advisers. So the individual who was there who happened to be an official of the International Paper Company was not there representing the paper company; he was there in his individual capacity as an expert on the domestic and international paper-making industry. (There were, however, more than one thousand advisers, and reality did not completely reflect the law.) The barrier that was supposed to exist between the advisers and the companies that employed them probably didn't exist in all instances, but by and large the system worked pretty well.

On sensitive political issues:

There were instances where we knew all along that we had a big political problem, but we went right ahead and did it. One was the injury test—the countervailing duty statute—which many people didn't think we would ever get. Another one was 'wine gallon-proof gallon' where we knew that we had a political problem with the domestic liquor industry, but we consciously went about acquiring concessions of a different kind that would help us in Kentucky and Tennessee in order to provide political cover for the delegation from those states.

Ultimately we wound up with the wine gallon–proof gallon people suing us; they became the most bitter. In effect, we had repealed the depletion allowance for the domestic booze industry. Most people were not aware of it, but there were a hundred pages in the internal revenue code that had been there for eighty or ninety years that provided very significant tax benefits and import relief—they were nontariff barriers—in the code for the domestic bourbon industry. And they had been there for a long time and nobody had been able to get them out. Well, we got them out by trading them away for concessions that were of value and interest to a lot of other domestic interests.

On the functioning of the Office of the Special Trade Representative:

STR became almost a clearinghouse for sorting out the issues and the interests and the process of pairing up concessions the U.S. was prepared to make with concessions that would give us more support domestically for the whole package. All of these things of course had to be—there was wheeling and dealing—but the basic polestar was, what is the national economic interest? Is this in the interest of the United States? It was a moving kind of target, because we had to take all the advice of these private advisers and decide what, where is the U.S. economy going to be ten years from now, twenty years from now. What is the value? I mean, if the Japanese offer concessions on steel or telephone poles in coverage of the MTN, that is of no value to the United States now and even less ten years from now. If on the other hand they offer concessions on microwave transmission towers, that is a value now, and will be ten years from now.

A good example from the Kennedy Round was the soybean bindings that the United States obtained from the European Community in return for, I don't know, something like $15 million in trade concessions in 1963. Today those bindings are worth billions of dollars. In 1963 the Europeans didn't know what soybeans were. They didn't know what an impact this was going to have on their whole common agricultural policy.

On coordinating agencies:

It was hard to get everybody talking the same line at the same volume. By and large, we did it, but there were exceptions. As long as we have free speech, you will never overcome that. But in the Tokyo Round it was less of a problem than I think it is in other contexts.

STR was able to stay ahead of the game, ahead of the bureaucracy. We were the ones who consulted with the Congress, who had the lead in consulting with the private sector; we had a special trade representative who was widely perceived as having the support of the president and access to the president—and who was respected. The fact that there is negotiation gives you the opportunity to pick up the reins and garner power in a way. It's probably more difficult when there is not a negotiation going on and you have everybody coming up and riding off in different directions. Or you have a situation where the STR is not thought to have the support of the president; or they create another agency or another interagency mechanism.

I used to explain to the Japanese that under our system the relative influence of agencies waxes and wanes considerably on the skill and imagination and dynamism of the person who holds the office. You know Henry Kissinger could be named head of the Small Business Administration and very shortly be running the United States government. Other people can be named head of the Department of State and very shortly be running the Small Business Administration. It's a scramble to stay ahead of the game.

On the application of the process to other negotiations:

In the trade context there is a constitutional reason because you have this shared power between Congress and the President. People have come to talk to me over the years about possible application to other areas in foreign policy. I don't know. I suppose in many ways it is applicable. The Law of the Sea, if there had been a fuller airing with the private sector of all the interests at stake and a fuller briefing of the Senate, then that might not necessarily have been scuttled. I don't know enough about all of this to be able to tell you; but it seems to me the elaborate multinational negotiations—there may or may not be more in the future, some people are skeptical about whether there will ever be another Tokyo Round—and the process of elaborate consultation and private sector advising may very well be a model for other types of negotiations. It probably ought to be explored.

Interview with Robert C. Cassidy, Jr.

Robert C. Cassidy, Jr. is with the law firm of Wilmer, Cutler & Pickering. During the closing phases of the Tokyo Round, he was the senior staff person for trade for the Subcommittee on International Trade, Senate Committee on Finance.

On the congressional role in trade policy:

Beginning in the late fifties, Congress felt that the trade policy of the U.S. was dominated by foreign policy considerations. This led to the creation of the Office of the Special Trade Representative in the Trade Expansion Act of 1962. Creation of the STR was a congressional initiative, essentially that of Wilbur Mills (who was at the time chairman of the House Ways and Means Committee), and was done over the objection of the administration.

The view in Congress that U.S. trade policy was not formulated to promote national commercial interests but rather foreign policy interests remained very strong even after the creation of the STR. A crisis occurred at the end of the Kennedy Round when the administration negotiated two nontariff barrier agreements which it brought back to the Congress and which Congress, in effect, repudiated. The first of these agreements would have required repeal of the "American Selling Price" system for customs valuation. That agreement was never formally submitted to Congress; the only legislative action was adoption of two resolutions saying that Congress didn't like the idea.

The second agreement was the International Antidumping Code, which Congress approved. However, the approving legislation stated that to the extent that the code was inconsistent with existing law, existing law prevailed. The result was that the code had no effect under U.S. law.

That confrontation increased the already existing congressional suspicion of trade policy formulation in the executive branch, and convinced senior members of both Ways and Means and the Finance Committee that the next round of trade negotiations necessarily had to be much more closely overseen by the committees to prevent the same kinds of problems arising in the future.

A second train of events which became rather important was increasing dissatisfaction, more in the business community than in Congress, with the administration of various import control laws, particularly by Treasury.

Those two sets of events, combined with the increasing importance of imports and exports to the U.S. economy, made Congress, and particularly these two committees, much more sensitive to trade as a political issue than they had been historically in the postwar period. This can be seen in the Trade Act of 1974. The most significant procedural element of that act is Section 102, which requires that any nontariff barrier agreement be approved and implemented by the Congress. Other provisions of that law require continuous briefing of specified congressional members about the progress of negotiations and disclosure to these members by the STR of confidential information about negotiations. The '74 act also makes specified members of the Ways and Means and Finance Committees, and their staffs, members of the U.S. delegation during the negotiation. All of those provisions were seen to be, and intended to be, an assertion of congressional authority in this area.

The purpose of the '74 Act procedures during the negotiations was to facilitate discussion between the administration and the Congress, or these committees (Senate Finance, House Ways and Means) anyway, about the merit or lack thereof of a given negotiation or agreement, to avoid at the end of the day a disagreement between the two branches.

On executive-congressional relations:

Strauss was much more comfortable with the Congress than his predecessors had been. He had many more personal friends in the Congress than any of his predecessors had had.

As a political matter he was much more sensitive to the role of Congress than his predecessors, and was more open with the Congress in divulging information about the negotiations and being willing to bring congressional people directly into both internal discussions of what policy ought to be and into negotiating sessions—to such a point that traditional tension between STR and the State Department, which had always existed, became much worse. This was because it was anathema to State to be disclosing to Congress what they considered to be privileged information about administration thinking on international policy matters. There was a series of battles between Strauss and State over disclosure of information to Congress, in which he always prevailed.

I am convinced Congress had considerable influence on various aspects of U.S. policy in the Tokyo Round negotiations, but one would have to go through each negotiation to see exactly where that was. At times, the influence would be more implicit than explicit, in fact more often implicit. For example, congressional "influence" would occur when an interagency decision-making group anticipated some congressional problem and made their decision on what they thought Congress might do—often without ever checking. Based on their general day-to-day connections with Congress, it was rare for the administration to come up and say, this is what we propose to do, what do you think about it? That did happen, but it was fairly rare; much more, an informal telephone conversation was the norm.

On House-Senate relations:

For all purposes during the negotiations we are really talking about only two committees, Ways and Means and Finance. The members of these committees knew each other reasonably well because they saw each other constantly due to their jurisdictions. There were many relationships among the members, although I don't know that many of them are personal friends. There was never any problem between members in cooperating to the extent they had to cooperate. They really didn't have to cooperate all that much during the negotiations, because there was no formalized procedure for approving or disapproving so there was no great necessity for the senators and congressmen to be sure they were taking the same line.

The committee staffs worked very closely together, again on a totally informal basis. There was definitely a conscious effort to maintain a more or less consistent line on the various issues at the staff level, because it was the staffs who carried out most of the discussions, and who were familiar with the technical aspects of the negotiations, which members were not.

There were inevitably some frictions between the two committee staffs because they are in some sense competitors or adversaries, but generally speaking I think the staffs cooperated extremely well. It was not unusual for one staff to say that one issue was more important than another staff thought it was. That was fine; it was a reflection of the priorities of their members.

By and large, staff cooperation was very successful. There was some difference in approach between the committees. The Finance Committee was more concerned about agricultural issues than the Ways and Means Committee; and was somewhat more protectionist than the Ways and Means Committee. Finance was probably more aggressive vis-à-vis the administration than the latter. That last point is perhaps open to some argument, but the Finance Committee was, and still is, a much more coherent group than the Ways and Means Committee—it is smaller, with a tradition of being clubby, whereas Ways and Means is very large [and] divided into factions, so that it doesn't work as a group as effectively.

Also, the Finance Committee had an extraordinarily strong chairman during the Tokyo Round, Senator Long. As a result of all those things, the Finance Committee was able, if it wanted, which it rarely did, to move very quickly and strongly in asserting itself on a given issue.

JOAN TWIGGS. *Did the members of various ISACs and various other advisory committees work with Congress in any way?*

CASSIDY. As individuals representing their companies and their interest groups, yes; as ISACs no.

TWIGGS. *Then their role was to advise the administration as ISAC. What did they do then as individuals?*

CASSIDY. Most of them did nothing. Most of them never talked to the Congress. A few of them, in their own capacity, not because they were on ISACs, lobbied Congress or just came up to talk about issues of concern to them. It is hard to pinpoint any particular sector as being more visible than another sector in this regard; it was really a matter of individuals. The issues that I remember people coming up to me and talking about were the subsidies code and DISC, agricultural subsidy issues, government procurement, and textiles, of course. That was all during the negotiations.

TWIGGS. *But was there any problem with people who were members of an ISAC and who had confidential information then acting on their own behalf for their company?*

CASSIDY. Well there certainly would be a legal problem if they were using classified information. I never ran across an instance in which that was going on. The fact that somebody is on an ISAC and is also on the Hill talking about his own interests could, in the view of some people, create some ethical problems.

On leaks of information:

I am sure there were leaks, but there were never any leaks in which I was the recipient of leaked information from an ISAC member. For one thing, I had all the information. I had much more than they had. But above and beyond that, no one had ever offered. Most people did not know that I had all the information. That whole system was kept very tight, largely because the congressional people did not want the world at large to know that they were sitting on all of the cables that went back and forth, because we didn't want a line at our door.

No, I am not aware of any leaks through the ISAC system. There was never a leak, period, to my knowledge, out of the Congress, which greatly surprised the administration, particularly in the State Department. The leaks of which I was aware were leaks that came out of various agencies, the usual thing: they didn't like what was going on, so they leaked the information.

On the congressional presence in Geneva:

In the intensive part of the negotiations, which was in 1978, there was virtually always some staff member in Geneva from either the House or the Senate, so that there was always a congressional presence of some kind.

What did they do? Basically, sat with the U.S. delegation in negotiating sessions in which we were interested or in which the administration wanted us to participate in order to have us speak up for the benefit of the foreigners as to what the congressional position was. There were literally hundreds of meetings going on simultaneously, so that congressional staff people could only participate in a handful. They tended to be the meetings related to subsidies, agriculture, dumping—extremely important to the Congress.

Probably more important to the process, the Congress staff in Geneva would sit with the various delegations and negotiators, in effect to shoot the bull about what was going on.

On the reaction of foreign delegations to the U.S. congressional presence:

Most of them didn't know Congress was there. The ones who did had mixed reactions. The Canadians were a bit suspicious—everybody was a bit—because the Congress has always been perceived as Neanderthal in American trade policy. Some of the delegations became fairly comfortable with it and in fact began to use it for their own purposes. There were occasions when some foreign governments refused to talk once they found out that there was going to be a congressional person in the room; they would not meet on that basis. That was rare but it did happen.

Most of the time the foreigners didn't know.

On domestic political process:

On the formulation of the Trade Agreements Act, the effect and role of lobbyists in general was almost nil; in a few areas, quite significant. In general, it was very minor because the process whereby the bill was enacted was in secret. Most of the political pressures which would be directed at Congress, Strauss tried with considerable success to divert into his system, the ISACs and his own special group of lobbyists that he created to put this thing through; so that Strauss made a conscious effort to try to go out and find the people who might have some problem and talk with them—or have someone talk to them.

In order of importance, lack of information prevented effective lobbying for most people unless they really made an effort to find out what was going on. Second, Strauss' assistants made most people feel they didn't have to lobby because they had their forum in his office. And it was a legitimate forum, it wasn't just handholding. Third, exceptionally, there were a few groups that did have an impact because they worked very hard to have an impact. They were, to my mind at least: the steel industry; a group that had no name then and is now called the Joint Industry Group, which is a group of exporting multi-nationals whose focus is custom matters; there was an ad hoc group of lawyers from the American Bar Association who had an impact on the content of the new legal procedures—they would be upset if you said they were lobbying, but they were; and there was the DISC crowd—they made a lot of noise but they achieved very little—and that was about it.

Now, you always had in the background of course the textile people; they figured they didn't have much to worry about, but they are shrewd so they kept an eye on it. There may have been some others but I don't remember any. Those are the people who took the trouble to get the information, formulate some idea, and then come up and talk.

On reasons for success:

I would attribute it to a few individuals and also to a fluke of circumstance. The individuals would be, in the House, Jimmy Jones, Bill Frenzel, Sam Gibbons, Barber Conable; and in the Senate, Abe Ribicoff and Bill Roth, and the fact that Russell Long let it all go on even though he didn't much like it.

The fluke of circumstance was that for a period of three or four years, by chance, personnel on some of the congressional staffs and in the STR didn't change much. It was very stable. The only significant change was people moving from the Hill to the STR, which didn't disrupt anything. So that you had, by chance, a group of ten or fifteen people who got to know each other very well. Given the context of negotiation and congressional implementation, stable personnel meant that the information system worked very well. It isn't just that you have the Trade Act of '74, which was the structure, but the fact that the central technical players were very familiar with one another.

Interview with Phyllis Bonanno

Phyllis Bonanno is the director of private sector liaison, Office of the United States Trade Representative. Immediately prior to joining the office in 1976, she was a lobbyist for the National Association of Manufacturers and worked on the Trade Act of 1974.

In 1977 and 1978, we met with the private sector 650 times and went over every single item that would be negotiated. We would go to them and say, this is where we would like to go, and they would say, we don't think you should do that. That actually was a negotiation itself, because one of the things we had to do was make people realize that when you negotiate, somebody has to pay the price somewhere. What we tried to do was make sure that not only were the concessions cross-cutting, but any compensations as well. As we went through that with the private sector, that information then came into the interagency process, which you understand was at the staff level, at the (department) secretary level, and a cabinet group.

At the end of all that we would then again go back to the private sector and say, this is what the government wants to do.

One of the reasons that the system worked so well in those days is because of what I call the accountability provision in the system, which was that if we did not take the private sector's advice on something, we had to go back and tell them that and justify it. It is one of the things that made the system different from most advisory committee systems.

Part of the success of the system had to do with the personality of Strauss as trade representative; Strauss really understood consensus building, and we are after all a consensus agency. We are not only a consensus agency within the government, but within the private sector. He felt very strongly that when you have a tiny staff and you don't have a lot of resources and a lot of time, one of your best sources is the private sector. They know what it is they want; and they know how to accomplish it, because it is what they do every day for a living.

On the structure of advisory committees:

Each committee was freestanding; nobody reported to anyone else. This was done for two reasons. One, we felt that a structure that reported up was going to mean that the private sector would not be as candid in those sessions as we might want them to be. There are also antitrust considerations that came into setting up this system.

When we first started all of this, there was great skepticism in the business community. The skepticism revolved around how you can really ever get anybody to come in and talk to the government— everyone knows that the government leaks. This also led to insisting that the committee be individual. That way we knew we could control what went on in that room, and one didn't have to worry about a draft report going on to another committee, or information getting out to someone else that a company might not want to get out.

Advisers felt that there was a positive ending for their industries and therefore were really quite committed to the process. You have to also remember that we do not reimburse either travel or per diem. We are also, I believe, the only advisory committee structure of this size that doesn't reimburse. So what you had was people giving their own time and money to come and work with us. That is a unique feature.

Now we have the opposite problem. We have many more applications than we have room for members.

I should also point out something else, which is that the committees were closed to the public under the American security system, which meant that we had classified minutes. Every committee has a designated federal officer, and it was that officer's responsibility to send to the interagency process an accurate report. The way you could double-check that was by going to the reading room and reading what happened at the session.

That worked quite well. That's another interesting aspect of all of this. But again, when you have accountability, it tends to make people more responsible.

On liaison with Geneva:

For one thing, we had to make sure that Geneva knew what the domestic constituencies were saying. That was a routine part of the process: Making sure that they were getting the information that was coming out of the interagency process in advance of any negotiations that they might be going into. Keeping all of that on track administratively. Making sure that the coming and going across the Atlantic really was working. Not only giving them instructions, but also getting back from them requests [for information] that they urgently needed to know before they went into a session.

Then as we got closer to the end of the Tokyo Round, we actually took the advisers over there—all the ISACs, the ACTN—for the big meeting. But it was not unusual for Geneva to send a request saying that they needed to know immediately what the soybean committee would do if such and such were to happen in some country.

Something very interesting has happened with the private sector system. We are almost in danger of a boomerang, because ten years ago we had people who didn't really know very much about it. Now we have people who know how to use the system. It is very interesting to see how this thing has shifted.

The process, as I see it, has been successful, so everybody said let's expand it. So we have expanded it. We now cover services, commodities—not just agricultural ones but things like tin, etc.—investments. Everybody thinks setting up a private sector advisory committee is the answer to all their questions. Well, it is not. The sleekness of the system is not there. The system has become slightly politicized.

I can't find the accountability anymore, because we are not in a round of negotiation. How does one become accountable for an investment policy and what does that mean? This is really something that we are taking a very serious look at there, because without accountability the system doesn't work. We are trying to design a strategy where, as we bring issues to the advisers, we set up a monitoring system of our own of getting back to them and saying, [policy] is not going to move in this direction.

Glossary

American Selling Price: A method of customs valuation established in 1922 to protect the then infant chemical industry in the United States. The ASP set the price of an imported chemical as that of its domestic counterpart. A tariff was then levied on top of the price. U.S. trading partners objected strenuously to the ASP and insisted upon its dismantling. During the Kennedy Round, U.S. negotiators did negotiate the removal of ASP and subsequent adjustments (i.e., orderly reductions) in tariff rates for benzenoid chemicals. Congress repudiated the results of the ASP negotiation. The experience with the American Selling Price negotiation was one factor leading to discussions of how to devise negotiating authority in such a way as to militate against post-negotiation rejection of results.

Antidumping Code: Dumping is an unfair trade practice involving the sale of a commodity in a foreign market at "less than fair value." "Fair value" is "usually considered to be the price at which the same product is sold in the exporting country or to third countries, but can also be the cost of production of the merchandise in question." (USTR, *A Preface to Trade,* 1982).

An antidumping code of conduct was negotiated during the Tokyo Round and implemented by Congress. A negotiation on this issue was also undertaken and concluded during the Kennedy Round. At that time, the U.S. Executive perceived the code as one that could be implemented via executive order without the need for legislative action. Congress however disagreed and disallowed the implementation of the code at that time. Along with the American Selling Price problem, the nonimplementation of this negotiated code caused U.S. trading part-

121

ners to have doubts about the credibility of the U.S. government in trade negotiations.

Codes of conduct: As related to the Tokyo Round, those international agreements reducing, eliminating or harmonizing uses of nontariff barriers to trade.

Common Agricultural Policy: The agricultural policy of the countries of the European Community. The CAP is designed to encourage trade among members of the EC and to discourage imports from non-member countries. Its purpose is to encourage European self-suffi-ciency in food production. It is also designed to promote stability in the agricultural sector, which in Europe consists predominantly of small farms. High prices are guaranteed for farmers. Imports are subject to variable levies which raise the price of the import to a predetermined price that will not undercut that of the European-produced commodity. Excess production is sold abroad at artificially low prices achieved through export subsidies. The CAP in the 1980s is under severe strain as member governments, especially that of Great Britain, demur about the continually rising contributions needed from governments in order to finance the CAP.

Countervailing duties: See subsidies/countervailing duties.

General Agreement on Tariffs and Trade (GATT): An international agreement to which ninety countries subscribe that regulates inter-national commerce. GATT is both an agreement and a secretariat. Developed in 1947, it provides for a multilateral approach to world trade as opposed to a bilateral approach. The United States acceded to the GATT by executive order. The cornerstones of GATT are the principles of nondiscrimination between imported and domestic goods once customs duties have been applied, and equal treatment of imports from all countries that have been accorded most-favored-nation status.

Generalized System of Preferences: In January 1976, the United States joined other major industrialized countries in establishing a general-ized system of preferences for the exports of developing countries. The GSP established a list of items that would receive duty-free treatment. In the United States, the list is revised annually. Certain restrictions apply; some generally import-sensitive items are exempted from duty-free treatment; there are provisions for removing an item from the GSP list once it has attained a specified dollar or percentage amount of market penetration. The GSP is considered in large part a development policy since its intent is to aid developing countries through trade.

International Trade Commission (ITC): The ITC is an "independent U.S. fact-finding agency whose six members and staff make determinations of injury and recommendations for relief for industries or workers seeking relief from increasing import competition." (USTR, *A Preface to Trade,* 1982)

Kennedy Round: The sixth round of trade negotiations since the establishment of the General Agreement on Tariffs and Trade, spanning the years 1963–1967. In the Kennedy Round, governments negotiated the reduction of tariffs via a linear tariff cut formula (also known as an across-the-board formula) rather than on an item-by-item basis. Following the implementation of the tariff cuts negotiated during the round, the average worldwide tariff rate was some 8–10 percent.

Legislative veto: The legislative veto dates to 1932. It was a device developed by Congress which evolved into a method of "checking" executive action in various areas. Thus, for instance, if the President decided not to accept a particular recommendation for relief from the International Trade Commission, Congress had delegated to itself power to override that decision via a veto and impose the ITC's recommendation. Successive administrations had contended that the legislative veto was unconstitutional, and on June 23, 1983 the legislative veto was struck down by the Supreme Court. At the time, more than two hundred laws contained some form of the legislative veto.

Nontariff barrier: Government measures or policies other than tariffs that impede the flow of international trade. NTBs may be intentional, i.e., designed to have a trade effect, or they may be the unintentional result of government policies that are designed for other, often largely domestic, reasons. They are difficult to identify, to evaluate with respect to their trade-distortionary effects, and to negotiate.

Organization for Economic Cooperation and Development (OECD): An international organization headquartered in Paris and composed of the developed countries. The OECD is the forum used by these countries to discuss trade and related matters and to coordinate policies on various international matters. It was set up in 1960.

Private sector advisory system: The system devised at the time of the Tokyo Round for the solicitation and consideration of advice from the private sector. Three segments were represented: industry, labor and agriculture. Industry and agriculture groups had both technical-level and policy-level committees. Industry groups were known as industry sector advisory committees (ISACs) and industry policy advisory committees (IPACs). Agriculture groups were known as APACs and ATACs (agricultural technical advisory committees). The labor sector was organized somewhat differently.

This system was devised in the wake of criticism about how private sector advice was handled in the Kennedy Round of trade negotiations. Participants on the whole considered it a good system.

Smoot-Hawley Tariff Act: This was the last of the statutes in which the Congress literally set the tariff rates on dutiable imports. It contained specific tariff schedules for over twenty thousand items. The average rate was 52.8 percent, the highest of the twentieth century. Senate action on the House-passed bill included 1,253 amendments, 1,112 of which were floor amendments. The Smoot-Hawley Tariff Act was enacted in 1930. In 1934 it was replaced with the Reciprocal Trade Agreements Act, which also ushered in the practice of setting tariffs via international negotiation rather than by congressional action. See Robert A. Pastor, *Congress and the Politics of Foreign Economic Policy,* pp. 77–84.

Subsidies/countervailing duties: This is a contentious trade issue. Subsidies can take many forms and there is disagreement about whether some forms of assistance to production constitute subsidies. For instance, is a program of aid to a geographic region a subsidy of whatever is produced there? If goods manufactured in a region benefiting from government assistance are exported, are those goods unfairly assisted in international trade?

The trade-distortionary effects of export subsidies are more easily documented, and it is export subsidies that have been the subject of trade negotiations. There is nevertheless disagreement over what practices constitute export subsidies. There are, more importantly, political problems in curbing the use of export subsidies, especially in the agricultural sector in Europe.

In the United States since the late nineteenth century, there has been a law designed to counterbalance the effects of export subsidies. It is the countervailing duty law. It allowed a duty to be imposed on imports that were determined to have benefited from a bounty or a grant. There was no provision for proving injury. When the GATT was agreed to in 1947, the U.S. CVD law was "grandfathered" so that it would not be contrary to the GATT (the GATT allows countervailing action, but injury must be shown).

A subsidies/countervailing duty code of conduct was negotiated during the Tokyo Round. While it prohibited the use of export subsidies on manufactured goods, it was not possible to negotiate strong language on the use of subsidies in the agricultural sector. The United States accepted an injury test to its existing law.

Tokyo Round of trade negotiations: The seventh round of trade negotiations held under the auspices of GATT and named for the site where the declaration opening the round was issued. The largest of all trade negotiations, the round officially spanned the years 1973-1979. The most active period of the round came in 1977-1979. The Tokyo Round resulted in codes of conduct governing the use of six nontariff barriers to trade, and resulted as well in agreements on civil aircraft and meat and dairy products. The six areas for which codes were negotiated were subsidies and countervailing duties, government procurement, anti-dumping, customs valuation, standards, and licensing. Reductions in tariffs on industrial and agricultural goods were also negotiated.

Trade Act of 1974: The act that authorized U.S. participation in the Tokyo Round of trade negotiations, that set forth guidelines for U.S. conduct and goals in the negotiation, and that provided terms for congressional consideration of the results of the negotiation. (It was reported out of committee as the Trade Reform Act of 1974, but later passed as the Trade Act.)

Trade negotiating authority: The authority for the United States to enter into trade negotiations with other countries is embedded in legislation passed by the Congress. The first act delegating the Executive such tariff negotiating authority was found in the Trade Agreements Act of 1934. That act was extended in 1945 and 1948. In 1962, the Trade Agreements Act authorized U.S. participation in the Kennedy Round of trade negotiations. When that act's trade negotiating authority expired in the late 1960s, the Executive was without such authority until 1975, when President Ford signed into law the Trade Act of 1974. Finally, the Trade Agreements Act of 1979 implemented the results of the Tokyo Round of trade negotiations, and extended for eight years the authority of the President to enter negotiations.

Trigger price mechanism: This was devised in 1977 as a response to complaints from the steel industry that the U.S. market was being flooded with imported steel sold at less than fair value, i.e., with "dumped" imports. This administrative arrangement was an attempt to meet some of those concerns, and to avoid imposing severe trade reprisals on exports from countries with whom the U.S. was engaging in trade negotiations. The trigger price mechanism set a base price (that of Japan's exports, since Japan was considered to be the most efficient producer) below which imports of steel would automatically "trigger" a dumping investigation.

Variable levy: The variable levy is a tariff that is adjusted to assure that an import will be priced at a predetermined "gate" price. It is used most notably by the European Community to support the EC's Common Agricultural Policy.

Williams Commission: The formal name of this study commission was the Commission on International Trade and Investment Policy. It is widely called the "Williams Commission," after the name of its chairman, Albert Williams. The commission was appointed in 1970 by then President Nixon to study the issues of importance in trade policy, taking into account changes in the world economy since the post–World War II period. The commission was to make recommendations for U.S. policy and positions in a new round of trade negotiations. Appointing the commission was one step in preparing for a round of trade negotiations.

Bibliography

Books

Curtis, Thomas B. (with John Robert Vastine). *The Kennedy Round and the Future of American Trade.* New York: Praeger, 1971.

Destler, I.M. *Making Foreign Economic Policy.* Washington, D.C.: The Brookings Institution, 1980.

Dobson, John M. *Two Centuries of Tariffs: The Background and Emergence of the U.S. International Trade Commission.* Washington, D.C.: U.S. Government Printing Office, 1976.

Graham, Thomas R. *The Impact of the Tokyo Round Agreements on U.S. Export Competitiveness.* Washington, D.C.: U.S. Export Competitiveness Project, Center for Strategic and International Studies, 1980.

Metzger, Stanley D. *Trade Agreements and the Kennedy Round.* Fairfax, VA: Coiner Publications, Ltd., 1964.

Pastor, Robert A. *Congress and the Politics of U.S. Foreign Economic Policy.* Berkeley: University of California Press, 1980.

Journal Articles and Essays

Bennet, J. Douglas, Jr. "Congress in Foreign Policy: Who Needs It?" *Foreign Affairs* 57 (1978):40–50.

Cassidy, Robert C., Jr. "Negotiating about Negotiations: The Geneva Multilateral Trade Talks." In *The Tethered Presidency: Congressional*

Restraints on Executive Power, edited by Thomas M. Franck. New York: New York University Press, 1981.

Destler, I.M. "Trade Consensus, SALT Stalemate: Congress and Foreign Policy in the 1970s." In *The New Congress,* edited by Thomas E. Mann and Norman J. Ornstein, 329–59. American Enterprise Institute Studies no. 305. Washington, London: American Enterprise Institute for Public Policy Research, 1981.

_____. "U.S.-Japanese Relations and the American Trade Initiative of 1977: Was This 'Trip' Necessary?" In *Japan and the United States: Challenges and Opportunities,* edited by William J. Barnds, 190–230. New York: New York Press, Council on Foreign Relations, 1979.

Destler, I.M., and Thomas R. Graham. "United States Congress and the Tokyo Round: Lessons of a Success Story." *World Economy* (London) 3 (June 1980): 53–70.

Diebold, William, Jr. "U.S. Trade Policy: The New Political Dimensions." *Foreign Affairs* 52 (1974):472–96.

Fisher, Louis. "A Political Context for Legislative Vetoes." *Political Science Quarterly* 93 (Summer 1978):241–54.

Johnson, Loch, and James M. McCormick. "The making of international agreements: a reappraisal of congressional involvement." *Journal of Politics* 40 (May 1978):468–78.

Kessler, Frank. "Presidential-Congressional Battles: Toward a Truce on the Foreign Policy Front." *Presidential Studies Quarterly* 8 (Spring 1978):115–27.

Malmgren, Harald B. "Sources of Instability in the World Trading System." *Journal of International Affairs* 30 (Spring/Summer 1976): 9–20.

Manning, Bayless. "The Congress, the Executive and Intermestic Affairs: Three Proposals." *Foreign Affairs* 55 (1977):306–24.

Marks, Matthew J., and Harald B. Malmgren. "Negotiating Nontariff Distortions to Trade." *Law and Policy in International Business* 7 (1975):327–411.

Rivers, Richard, R., and John Greenwald. "The Negotiation of a Code on Subsidies and Countervailing Measures: Bridging Fundamental Policy Differences." *Law and Policy in International Business* 11 (1979):1447–95.

"Symposium on the Multilateral Trade Agreements." Parts 1, 2. *Law and Policy in International Business* 11, no. 4 (1979); and 12, no. 1, (1980).

Wolff, Alan William. "Evolution of the Executive-Legislative Relationship in the Trade Act of '74." *SAIS Review* (The Johns Hopkins University) 19, no. 4 (1975):16–23.
_____. "The U.S. Mandate for Trade Negotiations." *Virginia Journal of International Law* 16 (Spring 1976):505–64.

Commission Report

Commission on International Trade and Investment Policy. *United States International Economic Policy in an Interdependent World.* Report to the President. Washington, D.C.: Government Printing Office, 1971.
_____. *United States International Economic Policy in an Interdependent World.* Papers submitted to the Commission on International Trade and Investment Policy and published in conjunction with the Commission's Report to the President. Compendium of Papers: Vol. 1. Washington, D.C.: Government Printing Office, 1971.

International Reports

Organization of Economic Cooperation and Development (OECD). *Policy Perspectives for International Trade and Economic Relations.* Report by the High-Level Group on Trade and Related Problems. Paris, 1972.
General Agreement on Tariffs and Trade (GATT). *The Tokyo Round of Multilateral Trade Negotiations.* Report of the Director-General. Geneva, 1979.

U.S. Executive Documents

U.S. Bureau of the Census. *Statistical Abstract of the United States: 1981.* 102nd edition. Washington, D.C., 1981.
U.S. Department of Agriculture. Foreign Agricultural Service. *Report on Agricultural Concessions in the Multilateral Trade Negotiations.* Washington, D.C., 1981.

U.S. Department of Commerce and U.S. Trade Representative. *Industry Consultations Program: Sector Profiles.* Washington, D.C., 1983.

U.S. Executive Office of the President. United States Trade Representative. *A Preface to Trade.* Washington, D.C.: Government Printing Office, 1982.

U.S. President. *Economic Report of the President.* Washington, D.C.: Government Printing Office, 1978.

————. 1979.

U.S. President. *International Economic Report of the President.* Washington, D.C.: Government Printing Office, 1976.

————. 1977.

Congressional Documents

U.S. Congress. House of Representatives. Committee on Foreign Affairs. "Congress and Foreign Trade Policy: The Multilateral Trade Negotiations and Trade Reorganization." Prepared by Raymond Ahearn, Analyst in International Trade and Finance, Economics Division, Congressional Research Service. In *Congress and Foreign Policy—1979.* Washington, D.C.: U.S. Government Printing Office, 1980.

————. Joint Economic Committee. Subcommittee on Foreign Economic Policy. *The Future of U.S. Foreign Trade Policy: Hearings.* 90th Congress, 1st Session, July 11, 1967.

————. Senate. Committee on Agriculture, Nutrition and Forestry. *Hearings.* 96th Congress, 1st Session, February 26, 1979.

————. Committee on Finance. *The Trade Agreements Act of 1979.* Report. 96th Congress, 1st Session, July 17, 1979.

————. *The Trade Reform Act of 1974.* Report. 93rd Congress, 2nd Session, November 26, 1974.

————. Subcommittee on International Trade. *Hearings on S 1376 (Trade Agreements Act of 1979).* 96th Congress, 1st Session, July 11, 1979.

————. *Private Advisory Committee Reports on the Tokyo Round of Multilateral Trade Negotiations.* Committee Print. 96th Congress, 1st Session, August 1979.

Periodicals and Newspapers

Congressional Quarterly
The Economist
National Journal
New York Times
Wall Street Journal
Washington Post

Other Books of Interest
from the Institute for the Study of Diplomacy and
University Press of America

CASE STUDIES IN DIPLOMACY

The Diplomacy of Human Rights
  edited by David D. Newsom
U.N. Security Council Resolution 242: A Case Study in Diplomatic Ambiguity
  by Lord Caradon, Arthur J. Goldberg, Mohamed El-Zayyat and Abba Eban
Resolution of the Dominican Crisis, 1965: A Study in Mediation
  by Audrey Bracey, with concluding chapter by Martin F. Herz
Mediation of the West New Guinea Dispute, 1962: A Case Study
  by Christopher J. McMullen, with Introduction by George C. McGhee
Resolution of the Yemen Crisis, 1963: A Case Study in Mediation
  by Christopher J. McMullen
American Diplomats and the Franco-Prussian War: Perceptions from Paris and Berlin
  by Patricia Dougherty, O.P.
Conference Diplomacy—A Case Study: The World Food Conference, Rome, 1974
  by Edwin McC. Martin
Conference Diplomacy II—A Case Study: The UN Conference on Science and
Technology for Development, Vienna, 1979
  by Jean M. Wilkowski, with Foreword by John W. McDonald, Jr.

SYMPOSIA ON PROBLEMS AND PROCESSES OF DIPLOMACY

The Modern Ambassador: The Challenge and the Search
  edited by Martin F. Herz, with Introduction by Ellsworth Bunker
Diplomats and Terrorists: What Works, What Doesn't—A Symposium
  edited by Martin F. Herz
Contacts with the Opposition—A Symposium
  edited by Martin F. Herz
The Role of Embassies in Promoting Business—A Symposium
  edited by Martin F. Herz, with Overview by Theodore H. Moran
Diplomacy: The Role of the Wife—A Symposium
  edited by Martin F. Herz
The Consular Dimension of Diplomacy—A Symposium
  edited by Martin F. Herz

EXEMPLARY DIPLOMATIC REPORTING SERIES & OCCASIONAL PAPERS

David Bruce's "Long Telegram" of July 3, 1951
  by Martin F. Herz
A View from Tehran: A Diplomatist Looks at the Shah's Regime in 1964
  by Martin F. Herz
The North-South Dialogue and the United Nations
  by John W. McDonald, Jr.
Making the World a Less Dangerous Place: Lessons Learned from a Career in
Diplomacy
  by Martin F. Herz

DIPLOMATIC AND CONTEMPORARY HISTORY

215 Days in the Life of an American Ambassador
  by Martin F. Herz
First Line of Defense—Forty Years' Experiences of a Career Diplomat
  by John Moors Cabot
The Vietnam War in Retrospect
  by Martin F. Herz
U.S.—Soviet Summits: An Account of East-West Diplomacy at the Top, 1955-1985
  by Gordon R. Weihmiller and Dusko Doder